ARE WE FRIENDS OR COWORKERS?

Exploring Relationships at Work

Curated by Changing Work

KEISHA WHALEY CHANTELLE DIACHINA
FAITH MCGOWN BHAVANI MANTENA
KHRISTINA KRAVAS ABRI KENIN CHRISTINE WENGER
CHRISTY SANDO BRIAN FIPPINGER EMILY RAEKER
NIYA BAJAJ CLAIRE WISSLER NICOLE ENNEN
HSIAO-TUNG LO KEVIN FRANZMAN ANNA OAKES
MARY MCDOWALL EREM LATIF LORI KIRKLAND
WENDY MCHENRY WEIKE LU ROHIT SAWHNEY
NICHOLAS WHITAKER SHELLY DHAMIJA
JULIA MELIM COELHO VINCENT SMITH

ARE WE FRIENDS OR COWORKERS? EXPLORING RELATIONSHIPS AT WORK

© 2025 Changing Work

All Rights Reserved. Apart from any fair dealing for the purposes of research or private study, or criticism or review, as permitted under the Copyright, Designs and Patents Act 1988, this publication may only be reproduced, stored or transmitted, in any form or by any means, with the prior permission in writing of the copyright owner, or in the case of the reprographic reproduction in accordance with the terms of licenses issued by the Copyright Licensing Agency. Enquiries concerning reproduction outside those terms should be sent to the publisher.

Editor: Lisa Thomas-Tench

Copy Editor: Joshua Humphreys

Layout: Natalie Lapre

Print ISBN: 979-8-9911984-5-5

Ebook ISBN: 979-8-9911984-6-2

Contents

Foreword   vii
Chris Reynolds

Introduction   xi
Vincent Smith

Deepening Respect

1. DROPPING MY SWORD   3
Keisha Whaley

2. THE NECESSITY OF UNCOMFORTABLE CONVERSATIONS AT WORK   11
Chantelle Diachina

3. BEYOND BOUNDARIES: BUILDING RELATIONSHIPS FOR RESULTS   19
Faith McGown

4. GOOD BOUNDARIES: EFFECTIVE COLLABORATION IN THE WORKPLACE   27
Bhavani Mantena

5. RED ZONE   35
Khristina Kravas

Cultivating Connection

6. VULNERABILITY: THE MEDICINE FOR CONNECTION   45
Abri Kenin

7. BUILDING MY HOME   55
Christine Wenger

8. FRIENDSHIPS AT WORK AND TEAM RESILIENCY   63
Christy Sando

9. WE ARE GROWING GREEN GRASS   71
   Brian Fippinger

10. PURPOSEFUL CONNECTION: FROM
    COURAGE TO POSSIBILITY   79
    Emily Raeker

Disrupting Disconnection

11. HUMANS BEING WELL   89
    Niya Bajaj

12. SUPER-CONNECTING   99
    Claire Wissler

13. A MYSTERY SOLVED   107
    Nicole Ennen

14. GOOD MORNING, NI HAO, HOLA, GUTEN
    MORGEN!   115
    Hsiao-Tung Lo

15. THE BROKEN SHIELD   123
    Kevin Franzman

Finding Purpose in Processes

16. FOUR QUESTIONS TO TURN COWORKERS
    INTO COLLABORATORS   133
    Anna Oakes

17. DEEP AND DYNAMIC: DESIGNING BEYOND A
    2D WORKPLACE   141
    Mary McDowall

18. GIRLIE, THIS ISN'T A FAMILY AFFAIR!   149
    Erem Latif

19. FROM FRICTION TO FLOW: USING YOUR
    HUMAN OPERATING SYSTEM   157
    Lori Kirkland

20. TRANSFORMING ISOLATION INTO
    CONNECTION: A PRACTITIONER'S GUIDE   167
    Wendy McHenry

Searching Within

21. FOLLOWING THE HEART'S GUIDANCE: A JOURNEY Weike Lu	177
22. COMMON GROUND ISN'T THAT COMMON Rohit Sawhney	185
23. WHAT REMAINS AFTER WE HAND IN THE BADGE Nicholas Whitaker	193
24. BONDING OVER SHARED GOALS Shelly Dhamija	201
25. FEAR OF SUCCESS Julia Melim Coelho	207
Notes	215
Untitled	217
About Changing Work	219

Foreword

Chris Reynolds

You can't build a relationship in a boardroom.

Like probably every one of you reading this book, I started out in my career as an employee, and eventually I became a manager. Later, I graduated to owning and running my own businesses. Over time, these businesses got bigger and more complex, but the way I worked with other people remained the same. I knew that I wanted to create and nurture a business culture that authentically valued my clients, my suppliers, and my team members: *everyone* mattered to me.

Why? Because—even right out of the gate as a newly-minted wealth management advisor—it didn't take long for me to recognize that we all have something in common. Each of us has a life story, and each of us wants someone to hear that story. We want to be seen, heard, and respected both at work and at home.

Business *is* people. That's why I genuinely want the best for people.

The challenge is that, most of the time, few people are actually listening to each other. Most of the time, our ideas and values aren't made a priority even when we're supposed to be building relationships at work. Some of the time, we even feel like outsiders in our own lives.

In taking the time to really listen to someone who's going to be involved in my business, I know they'll remember our conversation. The first thing I do when I onboard a new team member or client is take them out for dinner. Sharing food with someone is a good place to start. In connecting over a meal outside of the office, I see the walls come down. Instead of glum, work-oriented faces, people light up and share the best of themselves. I ask my team members to meet that same objective and offer a business relationship standard that's always a step above statistics and strategy.

What is the environment you want to cultivate? A relationship culture at work is built out of what's acceptable and what's not, and that starts at the top. An open, transparent leader who is genuinely interested in each person they meet creates a standard that permeates the entire team.

Who are the people you want to work with? A leader who listens is one who has a cadre of clients, team members, and suppliers around them who feel supported enough and valued enough to share their best ideas.

To get there, how can you build people up? To sustain your business aims, your ultimate goal is to *want* your best team members to replace you, and your best clients and suppliers to recommend you.

We *can* be friends and coworkers. When we build a higher level of mutual trust and we face challenges, we know we'll find solutions together. When we succeed, we can celebrate together.

Start with what matters.

Start with people. Listen to what they're telling you. Ask questions. That's where you'll discover gold.

Foreword

Chris Reynolds co-founded Investment Planning Counsel for and with the wealth management industry. More than 30 years later, his fundamental interest in people and problem solving remains as strong as ever. Chris explores opportunities in building businesses better through his Turning the Page podcast, and his new book, *The Six Circle Strategy: The Entrepreneur's Journey to Wealth and Freedom*, will be released in Fall 2025.

Introduction

Vincent Smith

Work can be a complex environment to navigate. It can fuel our passions, challenge us in unexpected ways, and trigger vulnerabilities. Each individual is unique, especially when it comes to why or how we show up at work.

In my 25 years' experience in tech I've found that most people are willing to sincerely participate and contribute once trust has been established and they feel seen, heard, and understood. I've also consistently seen collaborative teams deliver far greater results, and in more constructive and healthy ways, than a room full of individuals struggling and competing with each other. Here's a case in point: as a new program manager and performance coach for a B2B customer service team, I walked into my role and suddenly faced a lot of pissed-off people.

Customers were shocked and frustrated with the lack of support. Support agents were confused and didn't even know certain products existed. How could customer service be completely out of the loop? Why weren't service agents prepared? How could we ensure that customers received the support they paid for? No new-hire honeymoon for me. I had to leap into this and sort it out quickly.

As I dug into the details I quickly realized the breakdown wasn't about process, it was about relationships. The root of the problem came from a long history of conflict and confusion between the two organizations. It turned out there had been hostilities for years and communications had completely broken down. The product people were consistently "unavailable" and the head of customer service was always escalating. No progress had ever been made.

There was an advantage in being new. I could ask lots of questions. I needed to understand each side of the story, to know where people were at and what was going on for each of them. I was able to find time with the product team and offer them an olive branch.

As trust grew our dialogue deepened. It turned out that the product managers wanted to partner but they had gaps in understanding the customer service business and how to work with them. Customer service was in a panic and didn't understand the complexity of the product lifecycle or how to fit into their process.

With a clear understanding and a focus on building bridges, I brought together the key people and began to develop a team. It was important that I left "leadership" out of it.

We walked the product team through the customer service process, the customer experience and its challenges—helping them understand why we needed their help. They shared their processes and illustrated how complex and aggressive their work really was. As the two groups developed a shared understanding and language we really began to have a-ha moments.

In the end we overcame a deeply-entrenched stalemate by acknowledging each individual, building trust and eventually a sustainable community in which we could come together and collaborate.

This book is full of real-life stories like this one.

I hope that after reading it, you will find inspiration, new ideas, and perspective on how to bring people together and build your own community.

And if you need support in building a conscious community at

Introduction

work or connecting with people with the same goals, visit Changing Work, where you'll find great people, tools, and collaborative efforts, all focused on building better work environments together.

Let's do this!
Vincent

VINCENT SMITH

Vincent Smith

~

Vincent Smith is the founder of Quantum Leap Coaching, a professional coaching and mentoring organization focused on working with individuals through a uniquely compassionate, intuition-based approach to cultivate and accelerate self-awareness, overcome vulnerabilities, build resilience, and develop authenticity. His chapter "The Path Less Travelled" was featured in Changing Work's book *Leading with Compassion*.

Deepening Respect

A person who loves others is constantly loved by them. A person who respects others is constantly respected by them.

Mencius

ONE

Dropping My Sword

Keisha Whaley

What's your relationship to fear? Do you run from it? Hide from it? Try to fight it?

Could you ever embrace it?

I'd been listening to audiobooks for the better part of a month trying to heal from what I saw as the death of my business. On this particular morning, I was listening to Kristen Ulmer's *The Art of Fear* while brushing my teeth and trying hard to keep my train of thought from derailing. She was talking about how the idea that we should conquer fear was wrong and that, instead, we should embrace it with open hearts and curious minds.

I stopped brushing and pushed pause.

Ok, fear, I thought, *who are you?*

I SUDDENLY HAD a flash of a memory from one year earlier. I was with a woman I'd asked to perform a spatial cleanse of my office. I'd never considered doing something like this before, but I felt my world fracturing and was trying anything to prevent it breaking altogether. All I'd told her was the vibe was off and I wanted to clear the energy. She hadn't been there long before she asked me to sit down with her.

"I've been getting this message that I need to tell you to drop your sword," she said. "You've been fighting so hard to prove yourself."

I heard her words, but I didn't hear their full meaning. It seemed like there was so much to prove, so much to fight for. At this point, I'd been in business seven years and had just celebrated making over one million in revenue from an altruistic business model and no seed funding. I'd been told for years my business model would never work; yet year-over-year I'd grown in size and revenue. From the outside, it would be safe to assume I felt very proud and accomplished, but what I felt was beaten down.

"Close your eyes and picture the version of yourself that's fighting," she said. "Who is she?"

In the darkness of my mind, I saw a six-year-old me toddle forward, dragging the sword behind her. I burst into tears.

"What is she saying?" she asked me.

"She says she doesn't want to be abandoned."

THE WORK ENVIRONMENT I'd built was much more like a home than an office, and my team were my children—or at least that's how I saw them. Most were paid apprentices spending one or two years in the program before graduating. Because I was meant to not only employ, but train, I approached each one in the same way my mother approached me—shaping through guidance, encouraging development, and giving a voice in decisions. But I was also—at first, subconsciously and then consciously—infantilizing them. I referred to them as my kids. They affectionately called me Mom. I shouldered all responsibility and shielded them from any harsh realities. And this pattern, though playful, extended in destructive ways when I grew to lead a team of professionals.

My processes—from hiring to operations—were informal and friendly. With each new person, I saw their potential but was far more interested in what *I* could do for *them*. Though they all did their tasks well, I never gave them true responsibility or considered how they might support the business. I mentored the professionals like they too were apprentices—demonstrating first, then stepping aside for them to try their hand. If they didn't step up, I would do it for them. No consequences. No expectations. Mom will handle it.

I found myself unable or unwilling to set boundaries. I was involved in their personal lives. I catered to each individual rather than the company. I stretched our revenue to offer competitive salaries and benefits, paying myself below minimum wage if I even paid myself at all. I would forgive almost anything, accept almost anything, and in my attempt to keep people happy, sacrifice myself without hesitation as any mother would.

She says she doesn't want to be abandoned.

WHAT I WOULDN'T ACCEPT WAS that these choices I was so certain were making everything better were actually tearing it all apart. Every porous boundary increased my anxiety and depression. Every dollar I spent on perks and parties in the high-earning months was a dollar taken from a lean one. Each time I tried to appease one person, I'd hurt the others, and the more I allowed, the more they were forced to either take advantage or resent me. I suffered two diagnosed nervous breakdowns before I even acknowledged there was a problem.

This was perhaps the best and worst time for course correction, but that's what I did. I started making major changes to salvage what I could and to rebuild (or rather, build anew) what I felt was broken. I established a small team of my senior leadership to consult in all decisions, ending my family-table-style approach to decision-making. I brought in outside people far more structured than myself to help write our processes and enforce new policies to make us a stronger business. That was how I was able to achieve our million-dollar year, and of course, everyone was over the moon with appreciation, right?

Wrong. Very, very wrong.

Despite agreeing that the path we were on was unsustainable, my team found the level and speed of change untenable. It wasn't a growing pain, it was agony. Some felt the heart and humanity that made us who we were had been x-ed out. Others felt immense pressure that an axe might fall at any moment due to the rigidity of our new policies. Most lost their confidence in the business, some in themselves, and some in me.

We made it to the end of the year with a profit, but at what cost? So I let the pendulum swing again. The people I brought in to help were politely asked to step down. My senior leaders and I revised our policies and processes to be more flexible. I stripped away anything that felt at odds with who we were before. And, oh yes, I brought in a shamanic healer to bless my office. But sometimes there's no going back.

Some of what we experienced that year was due to the threat of recession. Client contracts were slashed in half or canceled altogether. Our largest client stopped responding to emails and wouldn't return our calls months before their contract renewal was to be evaluated.

Every month brought major losses until we were operating at just forty percent of our projections. I had taken out tens of thousands in loans and maxed out my personal credit cards to avoid letting anyone go. I was trying hard to bring in large revenue projects, painting on the face of confidence in every pitch while feeling terrified of the consequences if we didn't win it.

And we didn't.

By the summer, the senior leaders and I made the call to vacate our office and tell the broader team that over the next few months they would need to find other jobs. To do all I could to help, I had already written letters of recommendation and made a job board of open positions I'd found at other companies.

I delivered this message virtually from my mother's sofa. I'd retreated there on the precipice of another breakdown, hoping to find that same spark of insight that propelled me to write my business plan during a visit some nine years earlier. Being home and close to her would mean I'd be able to pull myself together and make a new plan.

As I was talking, I noticed an invitation pop up on my screen from one of my senior leaders and two of their direct reports. I had a vague assumption of what they might want to discuss as they were all client-facing and likely needed more guidance on how to approach this with their contacts.

Wrong again.

They were all off camera and only one of them spoke—though oddly not the senior leader. I was told they planned to start their own business and even had a name and logo picked out.

"We wanted to get your blessing."

At first I was just happy they weren't upset about my news. I told them how excited I was for them and asked the usual founder-to-founder questions like who will do the work, where do you plan to get clients, and what services will you be offering? Funnily enough, they'd been working on this for six months, had already approached the rest of my team and a handful of my clients, and had been working to adapt my methods to offer the same services. Even better, they planned to keep their jobs while they slowly built up their business on my dime.

I should have laughed in their little avatar faces.

I should have fired them on the spot.

I should have been on the phone with an attorney.

Instead, I said we'd need to talk more about it, but I was happy for them. As I ended the call, I turned to my mother who'd been sitting in silent solidarity and told her what they said.

"Are you kidding?!" she shouted. "They're stealing your business from you!"

She says she doesn't want to be abandoned.

I AM so afraid of abandonment in fact, that I would do a ridiculous thing like tell people who were stealing from me that I was happy for them. It took me a full day to come to my senses and request that they cease operations until we could meet and discuss the bigger implications of their plan. At first they refused and contacted another team member asking for our full client list. I was alerted and promptly suspended them and informed them they were in breach of contract.

Their response was immediate and severe. While emailing me with pushback, they were simultaneously paraphrasing bits of my communications to the rest of my team, telling them I'd turned into some kind of monster. I started receiving resignations by phone and email. I was asked to explain what was going on, but legally I couldn't say anything.

I was literally being abandoned, and I couldn't stop it. Any attempts I made to remedy the situation backfired and I was told by the spouse of the senior leader—who had only days before been one of my closest friends—that they didn't know who I was anymore.

It was the worst pain I'd ever felt, and it lasted for weeks. When it was still raw but months had passed, a colleague asked if I had come to understand the role I'd played in allowing it to happen. I was taken aback. How could I have played a role?

He must've read this question on my face because before I said anything, he said, "I'm not saying you *made* it happen, but how did you make space for it?"

It was then I realized how all those dominoes got stacked. Treating everyone like my child meant they could behave as such, including rebuking any onus for their actions. Fighting constantly and desperately to prove myself a worthy mother made it possible to take advantage of my weaknesses. All the massive swings to try to course-correct caused instability and made room for distrust. Some felt it was everyone for themselves while others banded together against the common enemy—me.

THE WHOLE SERIES of events was tumbling through my mind as I stood there, toothbrush in hand, staring into my reflection in the bathroom mirror.

This is what "dropping your sword" was about.

Now, I get it.

It's wishful thinking to reimagine the past, changing things here and there, looking for different outcomes. I try instead to take note of what went on and apply the lessons to the future, because I've learned by now that everything is cyclical.

No longer an employer, I'm dreaming up my own big picture. In this new era, I'm taking small steps rather than sprinting, as I see how my own sense of stability is worth tending to. Instead of trying to drown out my fear with avoidance, I've asked her to come with me, giving clarity on my blind spots. Though it was beyond hard, I thanked her for the chance to see that the biggest threats aren't in singular moments of disagreement, but when actual livelihoods are at stake.

When it's time to have a team again, I think I'll be ready to see them as adults with responsibilities to contribute towards—and who'll share in—the success of the business. They won't be my children. Their careers are not simply household chores. And I am not their mother.

Keisha Whaley

Keisha Whaley is an entrepreneur and community advocate in Dallas, Texas. Originally hailing from Oklahoma, she studied the Arts before deciding on a career in graphic design and marketing. While much of her work has been for noteworthy brands and has received accolades, she is most proud of the over one hundred young professionals she's had the honor to work with, teach, and mentor throughout her career.

TWO

The Necessity of Uncomfortable Conversations at Work

Chantelle Diachina

I climb the steep, narrow, musty-smelling carpeted stairs; each step reminding me I'm about to face an unpredictable event. At the top of the stairs I pass the reception office and head down the narrow hallway to the last door on the right. My heart starts picking up its pace and it's not just from climbing the stairs.

I knock and hear Kathy's cheery voice, "Come in!" I open the door and sit on the cozy loveseat across from my supervisor's desk. Kathy spins her chair around and smiles at me.

"How are you doing today?"

I inhale deeply and then I let out a really big exhale. "Actually, I really need a moment to collect myself. I just had a little fender bender."

"Oh my goodness! Yes! Take as much time as you need!"

Yup. Just before arriving, I sideswiped a parked car in an attempt to move out of the way of an oncoming car. The street was narrow, cars were parked on both sides, I was trying to be nice, and now here I am, sitting in my supervisor's office with my eyes closed taking deep breaths. What she doesn't know is I'm also collecting myself to have a nerve-wracking conversation with her that could very well go sideways.

The last time I had a conversation like this with another work superior was ten years ago.

I was getting ready for bed, standing at the bathroom sink staring at myself in the mirror. In the eyes reflecting back at me I could see the helplessness I was feeling and it angered me. Earlier that day, Dennis—one of the partners in the company I worked for—had another one of his screaming fits. In our open-concept office, there he was with his beet-red face yelling at me about my client who was not happy with a team member's work on their project.

I was just the messenger, but I stood my ground by firmly demanding he stop yelling and insisting we talk about it after he cooled down. I felt like we were on a stage in front of an engrossed audience of employees. Every team member had had at least one of these moments with Dennis, but no one ever challenged him about his anger problem. The last few weeks I noticed I'd been crying when I came home at night, which wasn't like me at all. Leading up to that, I grew tired and frustrated of being trapped in the cycle of complaining about him to my husband, which had gone on for several months. I didn't want to quit because I enjoyed the people I worked with and was rewarded by watching projects evolve from a client's idea to a tangible campaign that helped their organization do great work in the non-profit sector. But something had to change. I had had enough.

I looked deeper into my own eyes and stared hard. *I am never helpless*, I thought. Then the idea came to me. *I'll talk to him tomorrow and tell him how detrimental his temper is.* Outside of his anger, Dennis was a really good human being with a big heart. I've seen him teary-eyed after he's been touched by something heart-warming and he has always been dedicated to making a positive difference in our community. *If I lose my job over it, at least I gave an honest effort to rectify the situation.*

The next morning I requested a meeting with Dennis. That afternoon we sat down in my office.

"Thank you for taking the time to meet with me, Dennis. I called this meeting because I care about you and I respect you."

"Okay…" He sounded intrigued and mildly concerned.

The Necessity of Uncomfortable Conversations at Work

"Yesterday's screaming episode was a lot. Has anyone ever talked to you about how damaging your anger is?"

He closed his eyes as he nodded his head. "I'm well aware. I just get really frustrated and then I explode. That's just the way it comes out."

"Believe it or not, Dennis, I get it. I used to have a really bad temper."

The thought of this made him laugh. "You? The one everyone in the office has nicknamed Chill-telle? I don't believe it!"

I threw my hands up and laughed. "I swear to God! Ask my husband! Look, I know how hard it is to manage and I also know how destructive anger can be, not just for others, but yourself. I know how awful it feels to be angry all the time. You don't get to enjoy life at all. And from a health standpoint, anger is known to increase blood pressure, which can lead to all sorts of other problems. You're no good to us or anyone else if you're laid up in a hospital."

Dennis was silent for a moment, then spoke. "I know. It's just hard to work as hard as I do to keep this company going and to have to struggle financially because I'd rather see all of you get paid than take my full portion."

His words and presence felt honest. The energy between us seemed to have shifted from guarded to open and vulnerable. I paused, then nodded as I imagined myself in his shoes.

"That would be frustrating. I definitely see how many hours you put in. That would be stressful."

"Yeah, I'm stressed all the time."

"You've gotta get some help, Dennis. You're a good human with a big heart. You've just gotta be more careful about taking your frustration out on your people. Anger like that is a liability to the company that you and the other partners are working so hard to build. The way you scream and put people down overshadows all the good you do and eventually will push amazing people and talent out the door. No one wants to work somewhere where they are on egg shells all the time. I know I don't."

Dennis placed his ankle on top of his other knee, holding it in place while he pulsed his dangling foot back and forth. "I totally get it, Chantelle."

"Moving forward I just ask I am treated with the same respect I give you. And if you are upset with me we can talk about it like we are doing now."

"I can do that. It might not be perfect, but I'll do my best."

"That's all I ask, Dennis. Just… take good care of yourself."

That conversation went surprisingly well. I thought for sure I would have at least experienced the wrath of Dennis, but I didn't. I left that conversation feeling heard. I also felt empathetic toward Dennis's situation and happy that we were on the same page.

My conversation today with Kathy, however, was going to be a little different. I'm working toward completing my practicum for psychotherapy and the supervisor I've been assigned to doesn't seem to be a good fit. Her theoretical approach is on the opposite spectrum from mine, which means we clash on certain fundamental strategies used with clients. This was unsettling to me, especially since I was still a developing therapist. It was important for me to have a supervisor who could support my therapy approach so I could feel more confident using it. I was here today to tell her I intended to find another supervisor.

After I told Kathy the details of my fender bender, I took a couple of moments to breathe and re-center myself. I took a final big inhale and began. "Okay… what I'm here about today feels just as stressful as the fender bender."

My words rode on the back of my exhale, making it sound like I may have just been talking to myself out loud. Kathy tilted her head and furrowed her brow, giving the impression she wasn't sure where the conversation was going.

"Sooo, our first couple of meetings haven't been sitting well with me because it really seemed like our approaches clash. Skillfully sharing personal experiences that are relevant and helpful for the client is very much embraced by the theory I subscribe to, whereas it's rejected by your theory. Clients have all expressed appreciation whenever I've used personal disclosure, but through your feedback I feel completely shut down. I also feel the feedback you give is heavily centered on where I'm lacking. Constructive criticism is important and I can take it, but I also need to hear the areas I'm doing well in. I'm still learning the ropes. For these reasons, along with other foundational differences, I'm not feeling confident this is a good fit for my professional development."

I really wanted to shut my eyes and only briefly peek to see what her reaction was going to be.

I share these two stories because we've all encountered moments at work when boundaries have been crossed or a work relationship just isn't sitting right with us. We end up bringing it home: it keeps us up at night, affects how we show up in our personal relationships, and we grow tired of complaining about it to loved ones. We keep showing up at work each day, remaining silent or joining the commiserating club at lunch time. For me, the quality of my life is too important. Don't get me wrong, I know in some circumstances taking the risk of losing one's job in exchange for having a challenging conversation just isn't an option. Nor are such conversations possible with certain personality types regardless if they're a boss or a colleague—which is why not all challenging conversations end well. Quiet quitting is also a viable option, but when the circumstances are right, there's something far more rewarding about walking toward the tension.

I think about the outcome with Dennis. Despite feeling like our conversation went well and we were on the same page, he continued to have the same angry outbursts. I was really rooting for him, but I still had limits and boundaries to tend to. After three years of witnessing mostly other team members subjected to his rage, I ended up quitting. A year later we happened to attend the same community event. Dennis approached me and apologized. He told me he was sorry for the way he treated me and knew his behaviour played a part in my leaving the company. He also informed me he'd been working hard to change; seeing a therapist and starting a meditation practice. I was so happy for him and for our conversation. I gave him a big hug and ensured him nothing but good could come from his efforts. This moment made it all worth it. Perhaps waiting to have our conversation until I was crying all the time and feeling helpless was a little late. But a seed of change was planted through our exchange that benefitted many people. I am still rooting for him.

As for the conversation with Kathy, here's what happened next. Her face softened. She pondered a moment while gently running her finger tips across her bottom lip.

"First, I want to thank you for bringing your concerns to my attention. I'm really sorry I've made you feel that way. You are right, our theoretical approaches do have some key differences, but I don't believe they need to be antagonistic to each other. I really want to work with you and would like to be given a chance to address this and the way I deliver feedback so that it will be beneficial for both of us."

I'm not sure what I expected to happen, but it certainly wasn't that. I quietly exhaled the breath I was holding and felt my body relax. She went on to suggest a couple of viable solutions. I felt she was sincere and decided to give her another chance. I continued to work with Kathy and she did not disappoint.

About eight weeks later, I made a point to tell Kathy that I noticed and appreciated the ways she followed through in response to our talk; that her actions made me feel seen, heard, and valued. The look in her eyes was appreciative. My eyes mirrored the appreciation back. I would like to add that this conversation took place in the aftermath of COVID, the death of George Floyd, and the Black Lives Matter movement. It's not lost on me that having a white woman respond this way to a black woman like me was healing. The silence combined with the tears that welled up in both of our eyes affirmed this. I took the risk, it paid off, and this time I stayed.

We've since revisited how important that conversation was. It brought in such a deep layer of trust and respect between us. It fortified our working relationship, which after coming to a natural end when I opened my private practice, blossomed into a friendship.

It's worth noting that seeds like those planted with Dennis and Kathy don't always sprout, nor do we always get to witness their sprouting, but they are still valuable to sow. In both conversations,

The Necessity of Uncomfortable Conversations at Work

how we saw each other afterwards shifted to something more meaningful than seeing each other as just someone we work with or for. We were able to connect through the heart instead of just the mind and ego, and caught a glimpse of each other's humanity.

In both cases, I came into the conversation not just with what I wanted to say, but with highly intentional energy, which I believe is the secret sauce. I held just as much care and concern for myself as for the person I was engaging with and committed myself to that regardless of the outcome.

I believe in the art of dialogue; two humans exchanging thoughts, ideas, experiences in an open, non-defensive stance. I accept that all humans make mistakes and 99.9% of the time don't want to cause harm or make life difficult for anyone, so there was no need to blame, shame, or attack. I think the most important intention was taking the stance of not assuming individuals are aware of their negative impacts; even when it's so obvious, as in Dennis's case. Until I have spoken directly to them, I cannot assume they know something is bothering me. A conversation serves as an opportunity to expose the problem so that everyone knows about it, with the goal of reaching a positive outcome. The latter puts me in a position of having faith in the person I'm engaging with. I think they can feel that.

What happens after the conversation is the most informative part. It requires being unattached to the outcome and trusting that whatever unfolds will reveal the truth of the situation. By accepting this truth I am led back to my heart which will remind me that I am never helpless and I can empower myself by responding accordingly; which could very well help someone else grow.

Chantelle Diachina

Chantelle Diachina was an educator before evolving into her current role as a clinical counsellor. Over the last two decades, she has studied with various Master Yogis from the Sivananda lineage in India, Canada, and the US, which led to her becoming a certified yoga teacher, mindfulness-based corporate wellness facilitator and consultant, as well as a content creator for the meditation app Insight Timer. Chantelle lives in Victoria, British Columbia.

THREE

Beyond Boundaries: Building Relationships for Results

Faith McGown

The Great Recession not only tanked my thriving real estate business, it nearly destroyed one of the most important relationships in my life.

Hiring my best friend seemed a great idea when business boomed. When it crashed I avoided hard choices and difficult conversations by paying her from personal savings. The ending was not happy; the only thing my savings bought was time. Forced eventually to make the decision I dreaded, we both suffered. While the business did not survive, our friendship eventually did.

To be clear, my mistake was not hiring my friend. She was well qualified, perfect for the role, and contributed significantly to success. Instead our relationship, the friendship we had begun as teenagers, was not right for our new roles. When it came to work-related issues and frustrations I vented to her as a friend rather than as a leader and her supervisor. I also didn't leave work in the office during our personal time and activities. One of my biggest gaffes, one I'm not proud to share, was expecting my friend to support the business as she did me in our friendship. In the course of that friendship, Barb had stepped up to support me during challenging times and I did the same for her. Because our working relationship was our friendship, I unconsciously expected her to the do the same for the business (which in hindsight I can see felt like an extension of me). I was disappointed and even resentful when she fulfilled only her assigned duties but no more. And when the market turned and sales plummeted, I wasn't honest and upfront about the financial challenges the business faced—because I was afraid. Afraid of hurting her and afraid of damaging her family. Without clear boundaries, our friendship and working relationship were unclear, messy, and stressful.

Thankfully, because our friendship had been built over many years and was strong, Barb and I were able to move past the debacle that our work relationship presented. It wasn't easy and it took several years, but today Barb remains one of my closest personal friends and our relationship is stronger for having overcome such a significant challenge.

I entered my next career, nonprofit fundraising, with wounded confidence and an intense desire to avoid another failure. Another relationship-focused role, I recognized the need to create better relationships for work but still didn't know exactly what that meant or how to build them. Not yet a buzzy topic, relationship boundaries were essentially my next approach. Having learned the necessity of separating my work relationships from my personal, I attempted to apply that to my new roles by sharing less of myself. But while doing so definitely cleaned up much of the messiness that I had unintentionally created, my relationships weren't stronger. In fact keeping the relationships surface-level, erasing much of what makes me who I am and expecting the same from colleagues and clients, led to relationships that felt dull and less meaningful—and the work was still separate from the relationship. Healthy boundaries were a necessary first step but still not enough.

Additionally, I was still leaning too heavily on commonalities, albeit ones that were more work-appropriate than those I shared with my friend. What people have in common—interests, hobbies, beliefs, geography—is central to most relationships, and this is true of work relationships too. But it can lead to strong relationships built around commonalities that do not support shared work. As the stakes of our work relationships increase, so too does the need for purposeful relationships. Of course, liking someone and having things in common strengthens all relationships, including professional ones. But while they strengthen them they cannot be their core, or they might derail the business.

Asking for money—the express purpose of professional fundraising—is uncomfortable for many people, including those who do the work: fundraisers. Unfortunately, to avoid discomfort we often fail to be direct in the hope that our vagueness will avoid rejection. In doing so we unwittingly introduce doubt and uncertainty into the relationship. Ambiguous relationships are rarely productive and lend themselves to misunderstanding.

Indeed, it took me several years of not getting it quite right to understand how to do it better. As a major gift officer—the nonprofit sector's version of sales and usually focused on six- and seven-figure donations from individuals—I continued to build friendships even though I knew friendship wasn't my aim. "Transactional" also wasn't my aim. Less personal than my established friendships, these new relationships were still focused and built on likeability, rapport, and commonalities—sometimes ones that had nothing to do with the work at hand. Why? Like most of us, I learned how to make friends in elementary school and never really learned how to build other kinds of platonic relationships.

Thankfully this time around my too-friendly work relationships didn't cause problems—but they also didn't support success. I was an average fundraiser, performing well enough to satisfy supervisors but not achieving the success I hoped for. Until, several years into my fundraising career, I went to work for someone who at first blush I perceived as not valuing workplace relationships of any kind. She had little patience for the time I and my colleagues spent building them. Focused on closing deals quickly, she directed me to solicit in the initial meeting, a pace atypical to nonprofit fundraising: land the meeting, show up, ask for money, repeat. It was a strategy she had used successfully for corporate support and she expected it to work with individuals. My fellow gift officers and I balked at this brash and transactional approach and covertly resisted it, preparing proposals for initial meetings but rarely presenting them.

Despite my resistance to her directive, the pressure to move quickly was an unexpected gift. It revealed an alternative to pursuing friendships and forced me to focus the relationships I was building in a way I hadn't experienced before. With less time for pleasantries and little to no time for details that didn't directly support goals, I was able to facilitate better and more focused conversations without the distraction of unnecessary details. Up to that point, I centered my goals, the prospect centered theirs, and our conversations weren't necessarily aimed in the same direction. Now that I was afforded less time, focus became more important and the need to clearly identify our shared purpose became more evident. Building purposeful relationships not only led to greater success for me and the missions I support, it also improved the quality of my relationships. Identifying and centering purpose eliminates confusion and doubt, fosters trust, and improves outcomes.

In more recent years, as a manager to other gift officers, I've observed similar confusion around relationships and have seen vast improvements—in performance, comfort with asking for financial support, and stronger connections—using purposeful relationships. Many of us seem to have a sense of introducing the work after establishing friendship. Minus identification and confirmation of shared purpose, conversations, meetings, phone calls, and emails have no clear destination and can extend seemingly forever without ever achieving anyone's goals. Further, lack of clarity in the relationship leads to uncertainty, confusion and, in some cases, even distrust.

Here's what has helped my teams and me build better relationships with our clients and customers.

Identify a shared purpose. Purpose is inherent in all work relationships. In most cases we wouldn't be in a relationship were it not for the work. Identifying the specific shared purpose of our relationships within our work is an important and crucial step. Why are we coming together? What might be the other party's purpose? Where is the mutuality within that? As a major gift officer, the purpose of the relationships I build with donors and prospects is to secure financial support for my employer's mission. But that's not a shared purpose. My professional responsibilities are not what brought the prospect to the relationship. Despite goals unique to each of us, our shared purpose is supporting a mission that is important to each of us.

Confirm that shared purpose. Once identified, a shared purpose must be confirmed by all parties. Doing so sets the course and tone for the relationship, minimizing uncertainty and doubt. Initially this felt scary: will assigning purpose reduce the quality of the relationship? Will the other party be comfortable with directly addressing purpose within the relationship? Will I lose this prospect? These and other fears are not invalid. Indeed, there have been times when this conversation has revealed no shared purpose at all. And, yes, in those cases, I've lost that prospect. The relationship didn't progress, but like the push to move quickly, recognizing a dead end is also a gift.

After all, prospects don't support nonprofit missions—donors do. My role is not to collect prospects, but to secure philanthropic support. So while this direct approach has cost me prospects (or more aptly, has disqualified prospects) it has saved me significant time with the wrong prospects. Additionally, although initially uncomfortable for its novelty, addressing the relationship directly has always been well received and even appreciated, eventually leading to less anxiety and doubt for everyone. Determining quickly that there's no shared purpose, and thus no reason to continue building the relationship—at least for now—focuses my efforts on the right people at the right time.

Center (and re-center) shared purpose. Once shared purpose has been confirmed, every conversation and interaction can be structured around it as we work toward clear and agreed upon goals. The purposeful relationship framework improved my results dramatically. Within six months—much less time than the industry average—I secured a $1,000,000 donation, the largest gift I had secured on my own at that time, and one of the largest from an individual in the nonprofit's history. It wasn't a fluke. The same has been true for the teams with whom I have shared this approach. By reducing uncertainty in favor of clarity, everyone benefits. Most importantly, the quality of my relationships improved.

The approach has also worked remarkably well for relationships with colleagues. When a recent email exchange turned away from the work at hand and into tit-for-tat territory, I was able to shift the direction by acknowledging my colleague was upset and re-centering our shared purpose: "I understand your frustration and hope we can agree on [fill in shared purpose]." The simple but clear statement seemed to disarm the frustrated colleague, to refocus our communications, and to move the conversation toward resolution.

The approach has also served as an important tool for managing my own reactions and responses. When I felt betrayed by a colleague who changed course from the plan we had agreed to, and informed me only after informing senior leaders, I found myself avoiding her. Re-centering our shared purpose beyond this specific part of this particular project, helped me continue to show up positively despite disappointment and hurt.

Successful relationships in the workplace, whether with colleagues, vendors, or clients, must be centered in shared goals and mutual objectives. Too often we focus on strengthening relationships without ensuring they're the right kind of relationship. Friendly relationships are, of course, always the goal and having friends at work is not in and of itself a problem. The problem comes when the friendship becomes the focus at the expense of purpose. Meanwhile, transparently centering purpose in the relationship actually lends itself to true friendship. Efforts centered on the work itself, on the shared values that brought us together and on our mutual vision for the future, tend to deliver stronger results.

Faith McGown

Guided by the desire to align her work with her values, **Faith McGown** found her way to philanthropy following successful careers in journalism and sales. For nearly two decades her work has supported the missions of regional, national, and international nonprofits dedicated to improving health and increasing equity. Currently based in Dallas, Texas, she takes immense satisfaction in facilitating investment into work that improves lives.

FOUR

Good Boundaries: Effective Collaboration in the Workplace

Bhavani Mantena

Walking down the corridor into the designated work area for consultants at my client's office, I was focused on getting to my next meeting. Just as I turned the corner, *he* was there, standing squarely in my path. I moved to the left; he mirrored my movement. I stepped to the right; he blocked me again and fixed his eyes on me. There was no mistaking his intent—he was asserting power and testing boundaries I didn't yet know how to enforce.

My heart raced but I kept my face composed. "Excuse me," I said firmly, hoping that civility would diffuse the situation.

He did not budge.

I felt trapped and exposed in that corridor. My mind raced as it replayed the moment and I searched for the right words to reclaim my space without causing a scene. I did not find them. I walked away without saying anything but there was anger all over my face. I went straight to my desk and sent an email to the client manager that I was being harassed.

Later the client manager escalated the incident to HR. But he was prepared.

With calculated charm he flipped the narrative. "She wouldn't even talk to me," he said, painting himself as the misunderstood victim. "She was ignoring me."

He also said I was unlike the other Indian girls he worked with. The other girls were very quiet and sat in a corner and did their work. "But this girl is very talkative, strong and overly friendly to me—and I'm gay." Close to the client manager prior to this role, he was totally flipping the story to his advantage.

I was the only woman leading the project—a project with twenty male consultants. It is true that I am a strong woman and friendly to coworkers and collaborate with them to get things done. And I used to be flexible, working long hours and taking on more work when I was asked. I would never say no. I tried to be nice and friendly, but I did overreact with anger when things were unreasonable in situations like this.

HR asked me about the incident. I explained that my colleague had been intentionally distracting me for a week by calling my name from the back of the room for no reason, simply because I once asked him to lower his voice while I was focusing on work that needed my immediate attention. He kept making more noises; I started ignoring him. It was the kind of behavior that was inappropriate not only at work but even in personal settings. HR questioned me as though ignoring him was a sin. They were supporting his narcissistic behavior. But I tried to explain the context and I was very emotional in having to defend myself. I cried.

I watched in disbelief as my discomfort was overshadowed by his performance. They believed him. My voice became smaller, my presence was questioned. Is this all about who you know at the workplace?

I walked away from that meeting not just defeated but confused. How did he twist the story so easily? Why couldn't they see through his manipulation? Most of all I wondered why I didn't know how to set a boundary the moment he blocked my way.

I started questioning myself. *Why do people take advantage of me, bully me, or disrespect me? Why am I not able to influence people or connect with people?*

. . .

Good Boundaries: Effective Collaboration in the Workplace

I DISCOVERED that being aware of my personal space and my energetic space was crucial. I needed to be authentic, confident, and most of all calm. I had to start reading the room, the people around me, their behaviors, their energetic space, body language, and workplace dynamics. This situation was about alignment of purpose and energy.

I questioned myself again. *What was his human need? What was the significance of his behavior?* He needed attention and wanted to feel important. He was dishonest and disrespectful.

Was I being too friendly and nice? Was I operating from the fear of not being enough? Was I seeking validation? Was I my authentic self? Was I speaking positively about myself or being self-critical? Why was I not able to say 'no' to people? Was I being compassionate? Was I listening with all my senses to understand people and situations?

I found my answers. I was a people-pleaser. I was self-critical. Honesty was my core value. I was not being my authentic self. I was not self-aware of my purpose, my needs, and values. The result was that I couldn't read the room and so I was letting others get away with behaviors that I found completely unacceptable. I understood that my emotions and meaning arise from my focus and critical thinking. I also understood my unmet inner-child needs.

This situation was not about people disrespecting me but me respecting myself, my needs, values, and purpose. If I connect with my inner self, I can connect with others around me.

I was called to look inside and understand myself when I was confronted with a near-death experience. I suffered a sudden near-death health situation that was exacerbated by the internal struggles I had from several years of childhood trauma. That struggle was bottled up inside me because of not communicating my needs, values, and boundaries on both the personal and professional fronts.

The experience left me with a big shift in perspective. My journey to self-discovery began.

I started to understand how physiology can change physical and emotional energy for the better. All my life I had worked out six days a week. Healthy eating had always been a part of my life too, but the *why* was different now. The *why* then was to be in shape, to be healthy, to look and feel good. But with spiritual, mindfulness, and gratitude practices I discovered my true self and purpose. I practiced kundalini yoga and visualization and worked on my unmet inner-child needs. Conscious movement, breathwork, and meditation shifted my emotional state, and self-care for me now is more about nourishing the body with anti-inflammatory food. With these spiritual and mindfulness practices I'm able to connect with the higher source and myself, and that expansiveness has helped me to connect with others and to understand their perspectives.

There is no need for validation anymore. I am comfortable with myself. I am able to say *no* to anything that does not align with my energy and purpose.

FAST FORWARD A FEW years and I experienced a different incident with a colleague. He was from another consulting company and had just joined the project. The project manager took us all out for dinner. It was a friendly, cordial, and respectful group. Again I was the only woman and this new guy was overly friendly, sitting next to me and trying to joke and laugh with a slight touch. He offered to take me to the office. With my energetic space I was able to politely say no.

We all went back to our hotel. He tried to help me with my laptop bag and when I arrived at my room he offered to come inside to put the bag down. I politely but firmly said no. He could feel that energy. I could now communicate without any emotions and draw the line. The energetic boundary spoke for itself.

A week later he and I were the only ones travelling to a client's place and we stopped at a restaurant to eat. He asked me if I wanted to get a drink. I said I usually don't mind a glass of wine but I didn't want to drink alcohol right now. When we were back at the hotel bar he kept asking me to get a glass of wine. I said I didn't want to but he could get one for himself. He said he didn't like to drink alone and I could feel the energy around where he was going with it all. I had no intense reaction but firmly said no.

I was still confident and calm and let my energetic space speak for itself and nothing further happened that night. We were all able to work on the project normally, but I could see his attempted power plays whenever the client heard my voice more. It was all about giving credit to him, right? But it didn't bother me.

I was able to observe his behavior and listen with all my senses and could communicate with assertiveness and role boundaries. I give credit to my mindfulness practice for this clarity. Clarity is power.

THE QUESTION REMAINS: where do we draw the line for collegiality versus friendliness at work?

Many years ago I was working on a project with a government client, very slow paced and with a lot of resistance to change. It was taking 40 days to approve a contract as they had to go door to door with physical paper to get signatures. I tried to help them automate the process and develop a digital workflow for approvals and signatures.

The client staff were not cooperative as they had a lack of knowledge plus resistance to change. Some of them were disrespectful and it was a very frustrating experience. But the chief of that department saw the value in my work and how effective the process would be in terms of time and saving millions of dollars. So he championed the process and advocated the change to all departments to get the buy-in to implement the change.

That common purpose provided me with so much motivation, regardless of whether my colleagues were friendly or not. We were able to achieve our goals.

So let's explore where to draw the line with colleagues and where to establish expansive connections while not oversharing about personal matters.

It is important to maintain personal boundaries. Boundaries are limits we identify for ourselves and apply through action or communication. When we define what we need in order to feel secure and healthy, and when we need it—and create tools to protect those parts of ourselves—we can do wonders for our well-being at work and at home—which in turn allows us to bring our best selves to both places.

From fear of negative consequences and desire to please people, you should first shift your mindset to reflect and prioritize your needs and values. Recognize your personal limits, assess your current boundaries, and be clear on your priorities and limits. Clarity is power.

Now determine what your actual boundaries are. Here are the main boundaries I found to be the most important in my work life.

1. **Mental boundary:** What will you and won't you spend time thinking about?
2. **Time boundary:** How much time will you give to tasks, requests, and other people's priorities?
3. **Emotional boundary:** To what extent will you take on other people's emotional burdens?
4. **Material boundary:** How and when, or whether, will you use your personal property or finances for work?
5. **Physical boundary:** What is your personal space? Who is and is not allowed in it, and in what ways are people allowed to interact with you physically?
6. **Conversational boundary:** What topics will you and won't you engage in at work?
7. **Home life boundary:** What will you and won't you allow to interrupt your time with your friends or family?
8. **Role boundary:** When delegating work to others, how can you be clear on what you will and will not do?

Once you have determined your answers to these questions, define your "hard" and "soft" boundaries. Hard boundaries are your non-negotiables. Soft boundaries are goals that you want to reach but are flexible. Knowing the difference will allow you to make choices that are aligned with your deepest needs and to manage your energy as you work towards the others.

Finally, plan what you want to say when setting a boundary. If we leave room for ambiguity, we're open to people taking advantage of that. Clarity is also calming.

As I reflect on my life, I know that as a result of my childhood programming to prioritize others over myself, I wasn't clear on my needs and values and struggled to set boundaries. The result was emotional suffering and burnout. Once I was clear on my needs and values, I could assess the needs and values of others and respond to the situations instead of reacting to them. Boundaries are a self-care tool that helps visualize how you accomplish your tasks collaboratively to achieve team success.

Boundaries helped me to maintain healthy relationships while taking care of my well-being. You can do the same thing.

Bhavani Mantena

Bhavani Mantena is a business and technology integration specialist who works with Fortune 500 companies to help with their business transformation journeys. She is a world traveler and yoga practitioner who loves to hike and sail. She is originally from India and now lives in New York City.

FIVE

Red Zone

Khristina Kravas

I came late to the film industry.
Or so it seemed. I was 28 when I got my first internship, organizing vast piles of auditioners' photos for a casting director, juggling her incoming calls, and asking actors—attractive doppelgängers competing for the same role—to sign in for their auditions. I spent whole days watching them pace the tiny reception area muttering lines. "Can I help you, sir?" "Can I *help* you, sir." "*Can* I help you, sir?"

Next came a job in development and production, reading stacks of scripts, articles, manuscripts, and treatments in a perpetual search for the next big thing. I had a visceral understanding of plot development on the page and politics on the set. Both served me well. I grew quickly and adopted an identity that was a mix of naïveté and enthusiasm but not quite either. I listened. I rolled calls. I worked hard. I got promoted. And along the way I met people.

As an intern I accrued acquaintances who were, like me, blink-blinking at Los Angeles, trying to make sense of it all.

As an assistant I gained confidants, bonding over our bosses' temper tantrums and the generally disgraceful behavior that passed as appropriate in Hollywood office culture.

As an executive, time and shared experience turned allies into friends who could last a lifetime.

And as a vice president, the title I was offered within six years of signing my lease in West Hollywood, I made something new.

Enemies.

Reena, my first work enemy, told people—a lot of them: directors, actors, executives, people with power, colleagues, anyone within earshot—that I was inept and incapable. She stole my work, took credit for it and got me fired from the most rewarding job I've ever had.

Long before Hollywood, my first career had been as a professional ballerina. Colleagues weren't just friends, they were partners. We literally sweated together, and gave every ounce of ourselves in exchange for three hundred dollars a week and the chance to be onstage. We trusted each other, challenged each other, and felt bonded by our shared journey. Having an enemy felt foreign and unwelcome.

It still surprises me. How did things get so out of control so quickly? Even now, many years later, writing the truth of it stings.

Not so much because of what she did, but because of what I didn't do.

WORK ENEMIES ARE COMMON. The colleague who gets your promotion. The bossy not-boss who assigns you work despite not having the authority to do so. The *actual* boss who creates a list of demands that seems tailored to make you cringe.

Then there are broken-rule enemies, the workplace equivalent to the person who parks their Mercedes in a red zone. You see them sauntering out of the coffee shop, wiping oat milk cappuccino foam from their satisfied smile while you circle the block in search of a legal spot to stop.

Enemies are relationships that can break a career, like mine did, but they can also transform it.

Reena was a figurative (who knows, maybe literal) red zone parker. She didn't play by the same edicts I'd inherited from my mother, grandmothers, sister, society, friends. Those unwritten rules included: be subordinate but successful; be disciplined but easy to get along with; adopt amnesia about the value you bring to the workplace; and most importantly, be ambitious without ever showing or admitting that you are in any way ambitious. Squinch your nose in disgust when someone uses the word "ambition".

I was limited by rules of behavior that Reena had either disavowed or never heard of. I wanted to let subtlety and intuition guide me. I felt comfort in invisibility. I wanted to be respected and have my opinion sought out. She wanted none of that. Hollywood was a place for asserting your opinion and star-fucking—for competing and winning. If you weren't winning, you weren't bringing value to the organization and in her eyes I definitely wasn't winning.

The best I could do to combat Reena's figurative red zone parking was to meet her demands with indignant huffiness. I'd feign agreement and let currents of disdain leak out of my pores, lasering them in her general direction. As shocking as this is, it turned out that giving someone the stink eye—even strong, professional-grade stink eye—didn't produce a viable solution to the workplace drama. (I know! I was surprised too.)

Confronting her felt out of the question. Setting boundaries wasn't my strong suit. Confrontation however, is not necessarily the best first step when you're trying to shift an enemy dynamic. The first step isn't even a calm, cool-headed, heart-centered conversation. It is simply to stop blaming them, to make space for mutual understanding—or at least for something other than disdain.

It didn't matter where Reena parked, what starlet she was meeting for lunch, or who she was lying to about me. It didn't matter that she was acting out because she felt threatened by me and my abilities. I was so busy being mad and hurt that I couldn't see the root of my insecurities. And without that I was powerless. There was no conversation to have.

"But Reena. She's absolutely incredible isn't she? Super smart."

Having decided on an amicable, if sad, end-of-year expiration date on my employment, I was sent on a three-month out-of-state assignment in September. By November those days were nearing their end.

The speaker was a new colleague. We were mingling in a moody bar. A resonant hum from the busy restaurant downstairs gave our sagging and lightly-attended wrap party a hint of atmosphere.

"You know," I responded calmly, "Reena has spent the last year telling anyone who will listen that I'm inept and incapable. She insulted, humiliated, and marginalized me to the point that I was asked to leave a company and job that I have loved, deeply. So while I absolutely agree that she is capable, dynamic, and 'super smart,' you'll forgive me if I curb my enthusiasm."

I'd say you could hear a pin drop, but it was a bar. It was clear from my colleague's expression, however, that Reena had let her in on my incapacities. I saw a rapid recalculation behind her eyes. I was either on the articulate side of stupid or perhaps Reena had been... exaggerating?! Lying?! And if she was lying about that, what else needed to be reconsidered?

As though in a time lapse, I saw how I was able to shift someone's thinking about me. A simply articulated sentence had the effect of an earthquake. I felt powerful and vindicated. And I completely missed the point.

In enemy relationships, we go for the satisfying win, the ego boost that suits our narrative. "She's bad. I'm good." Victorious in our hour of defeat. This was the moment that I could have taken a second pivotal step and ask myself, "What am I getting out of all this mutual hostility?"

"Irritation, pain, suffering," might be the answer. Legitimate. Especially if the enemy is a bully. Beyond that, what we generally seek—and find—in an antagonistic relationship is real-life proof that we aren't smart enough, ambitious enough—that we're too cold, too warm, not likeable. Whatever internal language we have to diminish ourselves, our enemies are there serving it up, bespoke and uniquely tailored. You get confirmation of your worst interior fears and therefore an excuse not to be brave, not show your true heart, to continue hiding.

All I took from that conversation was proof that one needed to be morally questionable, like Reena, to succeed. And since I was too principled to do that, there was no need to succeed further—I could retreat back into invisibility and the relative comfort of not believing in myself, into overworking to prove my worth. I sunk back into the familiar pattern of being good but not too good, not attention-getting good—and believing that it was my enemy stopping me and not my own self-esteem.

I withdrew to a room with the glass ceiling I had constructed for myself and the relative comfort of not being a VP. Though it was a hit to my ego, it felt easier. We lose workplace battles not because we *have* enemies, but because we *are* our enemies.

Despite mutual contempt, Reena and I shared some remarkably positive qualities.

We were smart, energetic, accomplished, creative.

We also had positive differences. I had an ineffable ability to coax a story out from under the veil of not-quite-right writing. She had a breathtaking ability to sell it. I could be a source of stability and calm in what is often an exhausting and high-stakes work process. She could spark a party simply by entering a room. She was a loud force of nature. I was a quiet one.

One last step I failed to take in that moment was to ask: *Who do you want to be in this relationship?* What if I had taken time to define that? To carve out space for myself that also left room for her. Just think of what we could have done together if we weren't so busy throwing dirt in each other's eyes.

I've had more "Reenas" over the years. Different industries, different circumstances, different people altogether. They are every one of them challenging, connected, attention-seeking, intelligent, flashy—and they all have very fancy friends.

Thankfully I've got more tools to navigate these relationships now. I don't feel that same nagging need to cast blame or claim victory. My insecurities don't thrive on animosities like they once did. I no longer need to call my colleagues enemies... because they're not.

I accept that they shine bright and that I do too, in my own way.

It's not all rosy, of course. I still find it easier to fade into invisibility. And as for that last step, asking—*Who do you want to be in this relationship?*—I may be sorting that one out for a long time yet.

I like to think I may bump into the real Reena again one day. It will be on a sunny Los Angeles street corner. We'll have a laugh over our past. She'll reminisce about my talents in her characteristically boisterous way while I lean in and emphatically celebrate hers. We'll share a hug, and as I walk into the café with a grin, she'll stroll to her car. Parked, as usual, in the red zone.

Red Zone

Khristina Kravas

∼

Khristina Kravas began her career in feature film casting, development, and production, contributing to award-winning studio films and independent features alike. She has since spearheaded brand and marketing initiatives across a variety of industries, including luxury goods, publishing, and personal development where she helps empower students to harness their creativity, authentic presence, and full potential in the workplace.

Cultivating Connection

And as we let our own light shine, we unconsciously give other people permission to do the same.

Marianne Williamson

SIX

Vulnerability: The Medicine for Connection

Abri Kenin

I'll never forget how bright the fluorescent lights were, how loud the room felt, the smell of burnt toast in the staff kitchen, and the feeling of the medicine still coursing through my veins—all while in a lucid state of heightened sensitivity as I vacillated between worlds. Part of me was sitting in our company board room and another part was still journeying through the cosmos. My heart was beating. It was our company's weekly all-staff meeting and it was my turn to check in.

"Well, I just got back from doing seven ayahuasca ceremonies in fourteen days in the Peruvian jungle," I said. "It feels like I'm still on a journey and I'm not really sure where I am."

Did I really just say that? I thought. *I'm definitely going to get fired.*

I then proceeded to tell the entire company about the journeys I had experienced while on the medicine—the magical, mystical, and really out-there healing that had just happened. I had recently gone through a divorce and needed some heart healing for a difficult chapter of my life—hence the plant medicine journeys.

"And then the Green Tara, a Lakota Chief, the Buddha, and Jesus all showed up in a journey," I heard myself saying. *Abri, you have to stop talking,* another voice within me said, begging me to protect my self-image at work.

I've always been someone who goes all the way when I commit to something, but that many plant medicine ceremonies in two weeks was a bit extreme. Most people who go on this path start with just one then integrate that experience for months. I chose seven ceremonies in two weeks and their integration was going to take a while. For better or worse, my colleagues were witnessing my integration live. I paused and couldn't believe what had just happened.

Our organization, Search Inside Yourself Leadership Institute (SIYLI), born at Google, was created by a group of well-known neuroscientists, corporate executives, and respectable meditation teachers with highly regarded educational backgrounds. It was a place where I often felt like an imposter. *I'm not smart enough to work here,* my inner critic would often say. As a professional I get paid to be intelligent, to innovate, and to get things done. And I've just said I was doing plant medicine journeys and didn't know where I was? Oh man. I left the meeting feeling like I should start packing up my desk.

What happened next was just as magical as the journeys themselves. Right after the meeting a colleague came over and said, "I'm glad you shared your experience. It makes me feel more comfortable sharing mine."

I could feel my body relax at a cellular level. While it wasn't the exact words said out loud, what I took away was, *You're not alone. It's okay to be yourself and share vulnerably at work.*

Throughout the week colleagues showed up at my desk and asked me to lunch. Much to my surprise, I didn't get fired. I didn't get a feedback conversation. Nothing happened, except for people wanting to know more, including my manager.

This being vulnerable (allowing ourselves to be seen) hasn't always been easy for me. In fact, hiding has been a tactic I've used for most of my life to stay connected to other people. I came from a polite Midwest family and the message passed down was "don't disrupt the apple cart." By not sharing at all and agreeing with everyone, I could stay safe, remain out of conflict, and keep the peace. I could make sure no one got hurt.

Then the invitation to break free from this patterning came knocking on my door. It was 2016, right before I joined SIYLI, and I was part of a coach training program. At the time, I was in corporate consulting and completely burnt out from the professional mask that I put on at work. There was the me outside of work, and the "me" at work—two very different people.

During the coaching program one of the exercises was for the course facilitators to write a word on your nametag that they wanted to see more of from you. It was an invitation to be courageous and lean in—to play with the word they wrote down. I picked up my nametag. It said, "Vulnerability."

Ugh, I hate vulnerability, I thought.

Side note: One thing I've noticed is whenever I have a strong reaction to something it's usually a sign that I have some inner work to do. It was indeed an invitation—one in which the facilitators saw me deeply. To me vulnerability meant speaking up and I wasn't sure if I could do it. What if I said something that offended someone? What if what I had to say didn't make sense? In addition to safety, staying quiet was a mechanism that kept me likeable, and I liked being likeable. I wanted to rip off my "vulnerability" name tag and pretend it wasn't there, but I knew my integrity would hold me to higher standards. This was the beginning of a deeper relationship with vulnerability.

Fast forward to six months later, during my last interview for my role at SIYLI, and I asked the interviewer, "What are you not seeing that you'd like to see more of?"

"I'd like to see more vulnerability," she said.

Damn. There it was again—the V word.

I knew that by taking the job there would be no more hiding—that I would be saying yes to walking with vulnerability—that it would stretch me outside my comfort zone. But I wasn't here to stay small, I was here to grow. I could continue hiding and miss out on truer and deeper connection or I could show up, as scary as that was.

I took the job and the early days of working at SIYLI were

magical. Not because we had big salaries (we didn't) or because we had great benefits (we did), but because of the culture of deep and authentic friendship, built by vulnerability. We were a team committed to our mission and deeply engaged in our work. A team where leaders set a tone for vulnerability, where individuals were celebrated for their genius—and there was a mutual desire to grow together coupled with a deep appreciation for one another and our common humanity. We would eat lunch together, go on meditation retreats together, and hang out on the weekends. We were there for each other through life's most profound moments: promotions, births, deaths, marriages, divorces, miscarriages, and a global pandemic.

A colleague and I used to go for weekly walks together and on one of our walks we shared a deep personal conversation, on things that some lifetime friends don't even know about one another. At the end of the conversation I said, "I know everything about you, but I don't even know your favorite color."

This is how it was. We knew each other so well: our gifts, our triggers, our hopes, and our inner narratives that arose from our deepest wounds. We worked together to not only challenge growth and transformation, but also to remind each other of our greatness whenever we witnessed colleagues experiencing imposter syndrome, self-doubt, or other limiting beliefs. The healing that occurred inside the walls of this organization was deeply profound.

I read once that adult friendship is often built by several small moments of sharing vulnerably. I can think of many times when friendships were built in these micro-moments of courage, and here are some of those moments.

- A senior leader sharing that they don't know what to do and asking for help when we bumped up against a significant organizational challenge.
- A colleague telling a friend at work that they're not quite ready for a promotion, knowing that this deepest truth might be challenging to hear.

Vulnerability: The Medicine for Connection

- Opening the conversation on salaries as a company—sharing our salary bands to create more transparency and equity in the organization, even though I'm sure it felt uncomfortable for leadership to share this information.
- A colleague sharing about their mental health challenges and personal burnout—that they needed a break (which was honored).

So how did we reach this level of vulnerability? What were the routines, rituals, and daily practices that built this foundation?

This level of sharing only works in an organization that has a foundation of psychological safety and trust. I think what created that foundation were the routines, rituals, and practices that our leadership team built into the structure and fabric of the organization. These not only encouraged the vulnerable sharing of oneself, but did so with a frequency that made it feel safe and normal. Coupled with their own personal demonstration of vulnerability, this invited us all into the conversation.

While this list isn't exhaustive, here are some of the practices, routines, and rituals that supported our foundation of connection:

- **A moment to arrive and check in.** We would start most meetings with a "moment to arrive", wherein we set a timer and meditated together. Afterwards we would do a circle of personal check-ins and usually the prompt was, "How are you arriving?"
- **Mindful and empathic listening**. We would practice listening for feeling versus just what we heard. Instead of saying, "What I heard you say is…" we would say, "What I heard you feel is…" This helped us to drop into the heart space instead of just staying in the mind.
- **Meeting conflicts with curiosity.** Instead of shying away from difficult conversations to "keep the peace", conflicts were seen as a way to grow together. Conflict

was not avoided but met with curiosity and a sense of common humanity.
- **Leadership demonstrating vulnerability**. Leaders asking for help, sharing when they didn't know something, and sharing personal information about themselves, created a culture of safety and a feeling of everyone being in it together.
- **Self-awareness**. There was a desire to evolve as a conscious organization, meaning everyone was doing their own inner work and acting as a mirror for one another's behavior and impact.
- **Time out of the office together.** We had team retreats and a company-wide retreat where we would get together outside of the office for silly games, personal shares, and connection.
- **Desire to be non-hierarchical**. While I'm not sure we attained this, the desire was there. At one point two vice presidents in the organization got together and decided to get rid of their titles.
- **Appreciation and challenge rounds**. In team meetings we would do an appreciation round where team members could verbally share what they appreciated (about someone else or themselves)—as well as share any challenges they were experiencing. Honoring both the light and the shadow created a more authentic connection.

In sharing these success stories, I realize they may seem out of reach for many teams. I've worked at many other organizations where this was not the reality and in fact quite the opposite. Building a culture of friendship didn't happen overnight and there have and always will be bumps in the road. I also want to acknowledge the privilege that I have as a white cis-gendered person. This level of sharing vulnerably may not always be as comfortable or feel as safe for different races, genders, sexes, abilities, positions in the organization, etc. Our identities shape our experience. Living within the confines of our identities, our very existence can feel threatened depending on the way in which our sharing them is received.

I remember one time when a Black colleague of mine was about to have a difficult conversation with her white manager. I looked down at her computer and noticed she had two new photos taped to her computer keyboard.

"Who is that in the photos?" I asked, already knowing the answer.

"Those are my ancestors. I need them with me to have this conversation."

This is just a small example of how sometimes it's not always easy to speak up, out, or be our full selves when there are deep histories of not being able to be our full selves. We have a lot of work to do as a species to ensure that all people feel safe.

This raises the question: how can you be the leader our world needs?

As leaders, you set the tone for what's acceptable at work and what's not. Team members don't leave companies, they leave their managers. You hold more power and agency than you think. Regardless of your title, we all have a role in creating vulnerability and psychological safety. I invite you to reflect on the following:

- How can you show more of your authentic and human self at work?
- How can you encourage team members to share vulnerably?
- What routines, rituals, or practices would you like to put into place to support your team? How do you imagine this could create more connection and friendship?
- Where in your organization can you be an ally to individuals or groups who may not feel as comfortable sharing? How can you create more psychological safety?
- If you notice members of your team who are not as comfortable sharing, what can you do to support them?

How can you gently invite them in and create a culture of safety for them?

We don't need more robots at work, we need humans being humans—creative, compassionate, and connected.

Each moment in which we choose vulnerability over safety is a moment where we move from exclusion to inclusion, where innovation is born, where disconnection becomes engagement, where dormant talents become genius, and where masked robots turn into friends—where we move from a culture of "me" to "we." The benefit is real, both financially for organizations and to our collective human spirit.

By choosing to not take off the nametag of vulnerability and by choosing to move towards what scares me most, I have experienced richer, deeper, and more authentic friendships at work— friendships in which I no longer have to split who I am. So, if you weren't afraid at work, who would you be and what would you do?

There is no dress rehearsal for being ourselves. This is it.

Vulnerability: The Medicine for Connection

Abri Kenin

∼

Abri Kenin is the Founder and CEO of Core Consulting, a leadership company focused on human and planetary flourishing. With nearly twenty years of experience in leadership development, she provides transformative tools, practices, and experiences for individual and team well-being. Abri is an ICF certified coach, mindfulness teacher and a trained doula. She has worked with organizations like Google, Stanford, and Bhutan's Ministry of Education, fostering growth from the inside out.

SEVEN

Building My Home

Christine Wenger

I stood in the first house I ever owned with a mixture of awe and fear. A house I purchased in my mid-40s after relocating across the country. A work opportunity had changed everything. But now I didn't know what I didn't know. How would I take care of a home on my own?

I had always rented and managed minor repairs myself, but for anything big I called the landlord (or my brother). This was different. I was now my own landlord. I had to figure it all out myself or figure out who to call. Relocating across the country, leaving friends and family behind, starting over with two teenage daughters was hard.

What had I done?

The relocation involved many of our company team members. As many of us moved at the same time, this was a hot topic of conversation. *What areas do you like? Why?* 'What are you looking for?' changed to, 'Where did you move?' *Did you buy, rent or build? How's your commute? What doctor/dentist recommendations do you have?* As time progressed I heard stories of the mixed emotions everyone was feeling about moving, about up-ending families, and about pursuing new opportunities.

One colleague suggested I reach out to another colleague who'd moved into the same neighborhood a year earlier. I was used to doing things on my own and hesitated. Then I decided to reach out.

"You don't know me, but I hear we have the same taste in homes," I wrote. "What do I need to know as I move in?"

Back came an email with a list of things to do. First, contact Nick for any builder questions. Next, check the drainage in your backyard. Then install UV film on the garage window. Referrals for gardening services, pool maintenance, handyman, doctors—kept coming in. Our first big freeze (I was used to west-coast heat) had me on high alert: I got a reminder to drip my faucets.

Within a couple of months my daughter introduced me to a friend's parents who had also relocated. It turned out my new neighborhood friends and these parents were friends through work, and through the same place I worked. Small world.

My new neighborhood friends invited me to my first holiday party. There were the parent friends my daughter had introduced me to and several people I vaguely knew from work. We talked about the holidays, how our relocation was going, asked for more recommendations. For the first time I took a deep breath. My girls and I were going to be okay.

I hadn't given it too much thought in my 20s and 30s, so I'm not sure where I first got the notion that my professional and personal life were separate. *Friend* was reserved for those I met outside of the office and I didn't share much about my personal life with co-workers.

It didn't happen overnight, but after the move I noticed that I was different at work. We all faced the same challenges—getting settled, adjusting, rebuilding. This led to more personal conversations at work, discussions filled with practical questions, stories of joy and challenges, and the transition from trepidation to excitement.

I began to feel safer, bolder. For many years I had been holding back the growing stress I felt as a young working parent. I had been on a journey to heal and discovered my early warning signal for getting off the stress ledge. Yet I hadn't taken the leap to share that personal side with others. This new intersection of co-workers and friends gave me a sense of safety and connection that I hadn't known I was missing.

During the pandemic the conversations on video calls expanded beyond work. People and families were impacted in a variety of ways. Again I witnessed leaders offering a hand, creating connection and support.

Over time I've come to understand that friends at work are critical. Constant change, uncertainty, and workplace pressure evoke a scarcity mindset which in turn fosters stress and individualism over collaboration. But having connection with others fuels an abundance mindset and encourages optimism, compassion, and togetherness.

I polled several people inside and outside of work to form my new definition of a friend, and this is what I heard. A friend is someone you'd tackle the tough moments with—someone who listens, lifts you up when you feel alone, and shares a bond forged through challenges and hard work.

When looking back my most meaningful work memories stem from solving major challenges with others. Delivering a project under tight deadlines to avoid regulatory fines, tapping into creative juices with others to problem-solve, relocating family across thousands of miles, laughing over unicorns, crying over a cancer diagnosis, celebrating fur-babies and tiny human babies, graduations and empty nesting, designing an event in a week—hearing more and more stories involving the intersection of friends and co-workers. Whether delivering under tight deadlines, celebrating milestones, or navigating crises, it wasn't about budgets or deadlines—it was about shared experiences.

Sometimes we met the goal, sometimes we didn't. Yet we tackled the tough moments together. We gave grace when someone hadn't slept well or children were sick. We spent time reflecting on the work, especially when a major deadline had passed, and took time to celebrate along the way.

I no longer define a friend by location but by a mutual connection and a common goal. According to a University of Kansas study[1] it takes 80-100 hours to gain a casual friend and if you want to move into the close friend category you need 200 hours. We spend more time at work than we do with family and friends outside of work combined, and the key to making friends is proximity, timing, and energy. So for a friendship to take hold you need to be physically close to them, be at a similar life stage, and have a natural connect or "click".

Watching the power of teams that have this click and hearing stories from other leaders, I share three ways to fuel connection at work:

1. Unlock productivity. When colleagues feel valued and supported they perform better.

Being thrust into fully remote work during the pandemic was a jolt to the system. While the team was going through their personal challenges we had to rally to provide communication, tools, and support to the organization. It was a period of exploring and discovering how to connect with people in new ways while getting the work done. I saw individuals work together. The ideas began to flow. By tapping into their networks and creating new ones, the creativity grew. People were trying new things as an experiment and seeing what would stick.

Leader Action: Implement "stress-buffering" partnerships where colleagues check in on workload and well-being. Foster peer support through a buddy system and iterative feedback.

2. Identify similarities and explore differences. Leverage strengths and encourage knowledge sharing.

During my relocation I was reminded that we all want similar things: to settle in, to find our home in a new community, to provide a home for ourselves and/or family, to get back to "normal" as quickly as possible and live our lives. And at work I hear consistently that people want to do good work, be heard, and add value. The key to long-term team success isn't just working harder—it's working together. In speaking to other leaders and employees, it's clear in the stories that strong networks increase efficiency, problem-solving, and retention. When organizations invest in relational infrastructure rather than just individual output, employees and by extension their families and communities thrive. We are stronger together.

Leader Action: Create structured relationship-building through peer learning groups, cross-team mentorships, and informal meetups. Different ideas can include rotating meeting leaders, starting a meeting with an open-ended question, sharing tech tips, fostering casual "water cooler" chats, and organizing intentional monthly engagement activities around a collective topic.

3. Water the community garden. Integrate work and life through employee resource groups, volunteering, and shared interests.

When I introduced mindfulness to my organization, it helped make work life better and life work better. I've heard countless stories of how people were impacted by what they learned, and by being in community—and how leaders and teams flourished in new ways. Employee resource groups now use common interests to build skills and connections with others. Leaders have told me that mindfulness prepares employees for their next opportunity and that through groups or book clubs they've identified people they've wanted to join their teams. Something as small as a spirited conversation can show beneficial team dynamics.

Leader Action: Provide spaces for employees to try new things and build community—whether through organizing volunteer events, sharing traditions, wellness programs, or a special project. Friendships can transform workplace challenges into shared victories, reducing burnout and enhancing performance.

FUELING connection at work takes intentionality and practice. Supportive environments, shared experiences, and community, foster performance while easing workplace pressures. Workplace friends act as accountability partners, offering feedback and perspective. This peer support system can accelerate leadership development and improve team dynamics. Workplace stress is inevitable, but strong relationships make it easier to handle. They don't just help teams survive—they help them thrive.

After joining a new Fortune 500 company plus a whole company relocation, my views on friendships began to evolve. When going through a shared experience with hundreds of people and relocating families across the country, something shifts. Taking time to connect with others and having to get a referral for anything and everything—to really listen about what was going on with colleagues—began the shift to friendship. Some were friends inside work and others expanded to also be friends outside work. Having a common goal and a mutual connection fueled these friendships. I found who I wanted to be in the trenches with, who I was willing to share and be open with, and who I wanted to partner with to do great work. The more I allowed myself to be open and watched others around me, the more I was set on a path to work with people in a different way—to create space for them to share their ups and downs, which in turn created a sense of community within the place at which I spend many hours a day.

I often think back to that first day in my new house. The feeling of awe remains and the alone and scared feeling is now replaced with comfort, belonging, and gratitude. I have built my home with friendships inside and outside of work. I am not alone.

Christine Wenger

∼

Christine Wenger, a seasoned leadership coach with 30-plus years in Fortune 500 companies, helps leaders drive transformation through people-focused practices. Her chapter in her co-authored book, *Leading with Self-Awareness: Starting from the Inside Out*, explores her journey as a high-stress working parent. Her coaching and speaking engagements focus on mental fitness habits, conscious leadership, and work-life balance myths while sharing insights on how our brains shape behavior. Christine lives in Dallas, Texas.

EIGHT

Friendships at Work and Team Resiliency

Christy Sando

"So how long do you think you'll stay?" Rafael asked me cautiously.

We'd been at the company several weeks and were comparing our impressions. We were living in Europe and working for customers in the Americas, which meant we were working nightshifts and had limited opportunities to get to know our daytime colleagues.

"I'm not sure, a couple of years maybe. What about you?"

"Yeah, me too. Two years tops."

Several years later during a peer interview with new MBA students, I was surprised by a fellow student's reaction: "You've been at the same company over five years? You're ruining your CV!" Sonia meant well but I didn't believe her. I loved my job. I was surrounded by colleagues, many of whom had become friends. Eventually I joined the management team, and we created a place where people could connect, learn, take on new challenges, and work in projects with the newest technologies.

We were led by the founder and owner, whose leadership principles, openness, and compassion were ahead of his time. He assembled a creative and unusual mix—we were mostly liberal arts graduates: linguists, mathematicians, theologians, along with some computer geniuses. We were passionate about technology, exciting our customers, and doing great work. For our corporate clients, the experience was refreshing and unique and our contracts ran longer than is typical for tech service companies. Together we weathered many changes together, from the dotcom bubble to the economic crisis of 2008.

Our business meant constantly dealing with new challenges and technological changes. In contrast to the technology, the company's steady values and principles provided a supportive place to try new things and create meaningful work together. We helped our customers embrace new technologies and realize the benefits of innovations while also helping teams adopt, grow, and improve their work using new tools.

Why would I leave that just to have a model CV? In the end I stayed with the company for nearly eighteen happy years. And Rafael? He's still there today, along with many others from those early days.

Looking for something new, then disruption

In the end the decision to leave wasn't easy, but I had become curious and wanted to see something new—to continue learning in a different company. I chose to work in business development with the founder of a young tech start up. They had just received a 40-million-dollar growth equity investment, which promised to be a stark contrast to the owner-operated and organically grown company I knew so well. Things move notoriously fast in tech start-ups, and with this new investment it was clear we were in for a ride. When COVID-19 hit, demands on our business only increased as companies scurried to digitize processes.

I was only a few months into my new role on the morning I went to the office to retrieve my equipment so I could move into my home office. It was a week before the official lockdown began in Germany. The streets were eerily quiet for a weekday morning. No one was certain how long this would last and no one knew then how much quieter the streets would become. Now when I think back on that time I often take a deep breath and remind myself: *that really happened.*

Some of our customers experienced setbacks but overall, business was booming. COVID-19 drove digitalization like no CIO ever could. I felt lucky to be able to continue work. Many people couldn't as businesses shuttered. Worse yet, many lost loved ones as well. As work moved to home I was even more grateful for having worked decades for a company with a specialty in online collaboration and remote work. But at this new company these skills were far from usual. Our days were packed with online meetings and although it seemed we were talking more than ever, I was missing personal connection and meaningful conversations. The days became a bit of a blur—six to eight hours of calls and most other waking hours filled with the work of following up and planning.

Still feeling fresh to the company, and with new hires joining every month, I was longing to get to know people and to navigate the organization. To best serve our business partners, I needed successful connections to nearly every department.

Intentional connection, a form of friendship

There was hardly a chance for any meaningful connection in those long and oversized meetings. It was impossible to get to know people outside the agendas and to-do lists. There was no space to just *be*. I couldn't look forward to bumping into a data analyst on the bus to work, or to catching the user experience designers in the kitchen and hearing about their work. Connecting to colleagues would have to be very intentional.

I started to schedule short coffee breaks throughout the week with people from different areas of the company. There I could hear what they were working on and could share what we were doing to grow the partner business. This made our work come alive for me, and when I heard company reports I knew who was behind those achieved targets and what it took to get there.

Being in touch also allowed us to share the struggles we were having. Apartments suddenly feeling too small when accommodating a workspace. Children popping up in video calls. Many of us live in Germany but aren't from here, and were feeling further than ever from our extended families. Some people were even stranded abroad, on holiday when the pandemic brought the world to a halt.

I was feeling trapped and untethered all at once. I'd always had the privilege of being able to jump on a plane anytime I was needed by family in the United States, where I grew up. It didn't happen often, but in the handful of unforeseen times that I needed to be there, I showed up. It was a comfort to know that that possibility existed. When international flights were cancelled I started to question myself, wondering what ever compelled me to move here so many years ago. *What was I doing here?*

I researched and found an eight-week online course called Mindful Self-Compassion, which calmed me and taught me to recognize things as they are without the cruel stories and judgement that my mind often adds. Later I was longing for a way to bring mindfulness and business together, and was happy to join the Inner MBA program and the online community it has created.

When we were past the worst of the pandemic I could see how the inner and interpersonal work I'd done was rewarding me again and again. In one meeting, we were stuck needing information about our product. I suggested we chat to a particular developer, as my interactions with her made me believe we'd get a quick and straight answer. The reaction of the others stunned me: "She never answers my chats."

I know key people in this company are often bombarded with questions, I was thinking. In this case I chatted to her, received the answer, and we moved forward with our planning. The difference between getting a reply or not is whether it's appreciated, acknowledged, and reciprocated. If I struggled to find information or understand a decision, I knew whom I could ask—and when a technician wanted a business perspective or a partner opinion on a new feature, I was available to help. When later that developer left the company I made it a point to have a coffee with her again. She thanked me especially for taking time to explain our partner business to her and for recognizing her input and expertise in front of our associates. The connections we made eased work tremendously and added meaning to our projects. No matter how busy we were, we made time for each other and showed up—just like friends do.

I've lived abroad and worked in international settings nearly my entire career. Being from the midwestern United States I'm aware I may have a predisposition to friendliness, and I'm also attentive to intercultural interpretations of it. Friendly behavior can make others suspicious of my intentions or question my sincerity. I've found the best way to deal with any doubts is to be authentic and honest. Reliability speaks for itself.

What friendships and resilient teams share

Showing up with curiosity, empathy, trust, and vulnerability—and treating myself and others the way I'd treat a friend—became skills for me. Some of the bonds I made on the job were centered solely around the business. Former colleagues have reached out years later asking for advice about something they're working on. Other connections flourished into friendships outside of work and we're still in contact despite moves or changes in jobs. Friendship can have many layers, and what interests me is the connection between friendships and resilient teams.

The idea that we're living in a world that's volatile, uncertain, complex, and ambiguous is not new. Businesses change and technology evolves so rapidly that old ways of working with or relying on data can't help us predict nor prepare for the future. In recent years there have been numerous disruptions in society, technology, economics, and politics—which together make a strong case for building resilient and adaptable teams that can pivot and perform well even during changes and transitions. The pandemic was one shocking example of this, and one that affected us all. If we practice friendship in all our relationships, the sense of connection can provide the resources to navigate and adapt to disruption with greater ease.

There are several articles about what makes a good friendship, and many studies on building high-performing teams or increasing team effectiveness. What I find interesting is how much the two have in common. I've brought together some of the key aspects which I invite you to reflect upon, both in terms of a friendship and as a team in a work setting:

- Respectful and well-intentioned: Treating people with respect is easy when we truly believe that we all show up to do our best work.
- Psychological safety: If something is going wrong, psychological safety allows us to talk about difficulties early. We know we can make mistakes and still be valuable to the team.
- Trustworthy, reliable, dependable: We take responsibility and commit. We do what we say we will.
- Listening, empathy: Be curious. Create space for others to express their ideas and contribute their perspective.
- Helpful, supporting others: Elevate the people around you and they will be there for you in return.
- Common interests, values, shared goals: Our work takes on new meaning when we have common interests and goals.
- Shared understanding of team structure and roles: In friendship terms, this is synonymous with having healthy boundaries.

Given these points, I think there's a good case for fostering friendships at work. We don't have to be best friends in all areas of life but being friendly and intentional about connecting with others creates resilient teams at work. When we make a connection and feel like we belong, it helps us show up as whole and authentic people and allows others to do the same. Ideally these connections are possible and supported throughout the company and extended to business partners. But even if this isn't the case, I find it's still possible through setting my own intention for personal interactions.

For me, friendship at work means connecting with others and understanding that we all bring our own mix of characteristics: talents, abilities, strengths, fears, needs, etc. We come together to accomplish something we couldn't achieve on our own and we seek meaningful work. If we can show up as our true selves to make genuine connections with our coworkers, we build trust and a sense of belonging that help us weather difficult times and inevitable changes.

More important than how long you stay at a company is how you show up, and the connections you develop there.

Christy Sando

∽

Christy Sando is an accomplished executive with extensive experience in management and in growing innovative tech companies in international settings. She has led strategic initiatives in driving organizational growth and fostering high-performance teams. With a strong focus on conscious leadership and continuous improvement, she is a certified business coach and change management consultant. She empowers individuals, builds collaborative communities, and creates lasting business impact.

NINE

We Are Growing Green Grass

Brian Fippinger

So my wife wanted to write a book. I knew that my wife *needed* to write the book. It was a book she was uniquely qualified to write and a message I knew corporate leaders needed to hear. But writing a book is hard work, long hours of research and writing and editing and editing and writing, and... you get the idea. So we decided that in order to give her the space to do this work, I would leave our small coaching and consulting firm and go back out to the real world to ensure we had enough money coming in to pay our bills and insurance.

That meant I needed to do something I hadn't done for a long time.

Look for a job.

Luckily I'm at the point in my career where I have many connections to call on, and I was introduced to several companies with open positions where my experience would be a fit.

That of course meant I had to endure the worst part of any job search: the interviews. I went through several before I got to one that was very interesting. It was with a $70 billion global company. Not that the job was that exciting at face value. It was a role I had performed many times in the past. It was the interview that was interesting.

During the five-interview process, I met with co-workers, my boss, and executives from the groups that I would be interacting with on a daily basis. I even interviewed the division's Executive Director.

Sounds pretty standard fare, right? It wasn't.

You see, my last question in every job interview of my 46-year career had always been the same: "Where is the brown grass? You've told me all about the green grass; where is the *brown* grass? I know there is always brown grass."

In my experience the interview process was as much about selling the opportunity to me as it was about getting information from me. But this time I didn't have to ask that question during any of the interviews. Everyone I spoke to, including the executive director, *led* with the brown grass. Their honesty was as refreshing as it was startling.

And they were not lying. They may have been rather underplaying it. The common description of the organization used during the interviews was "an adolescent." In reality it was an infant. There was a lot of brown grass.

The few processes in place were hidden inside the individual minds of those doing the work. The formal training for the role had nothing to do with the role itself. Halfway through the second day the instructor told me, "Why don't you just skip the rest of this course. Nothing in the material will pertain to what you do."

For the next few months the only guidance I got was from the teammate who had been assigned as my mentor (who was a tremendous help). Beside him, I was left out on the island. When I asked my boss her typical response was, "Did you ask Ray?"

In addition the regional director of the group I was supporting in my role bluntly told me, "We don't trust your organization at all."

As if this wasn't enough, the manager who hired me left the company—an occurrence that would happen six more times in the four-and-a-half-year period of this story.

Then one day I got invited to an after-hours meeting from an oddly named Teams group comprised of many of my team members whom I'd seen in meetings but had never spoken to one-on-one. It turned out that for a long time this group had been meeting every other week for a virtual drink. The group was cross-generational—the youngest was not yet 30 and I, the oldest, was 62. It was culturally diverse too, and I learned that its purpose was to gather around a virtual bar in order to complain about work. It was a fun group, and gave everyone the chance to get to know each other a little better. But it did nothing to help solve the many issues we were facing.

Then one day one of us had an issue with a customer that they weren't sure how to handle. Instead of doing what we usually did—trying to figure it out by ourselves or pinging individuals whom we thought might know—the colleague created a Teams chat with four of us and shared the issue with the group. Shortly there was a lively back-and-forth with ideas, with other people in other departments who might be able to help, and with the clarification of questions that got into not only the how of solving the issue at hand but also how to stop it from happening again.

It was the first instance of what's now a multiple-times-a-day occurrence. The group was christened The Bunch and quickly became the go-to group when anyone needed help, ideas, or just a chat. After adding several more individuals to The Bunch we decided to re-initiate the monthly after-work meetings for drinks with this smaller group, only with some guardrails around it. First, no talk of work was allowed. None. This was a time to get away from work, to get to really know each other, and to relax.

Most of the time we have an initial semi-facilitated time, by which I mean someone asks questions like, "What's the best Christmas gift you have ever received?" or, "What was your favorite job you've ever had?" Sharing like this has not only brought The Bunch closer but has led to deeper discussions that have informed and enlightened all of us.

Several important things have grown organically from this closeness. One is that when a new person joins the team, The Bunch makes sure they're shown how to do things and not left on an island—that they know they have a group of people they can come to for help, either through a group team chat or directly to one of us.

I am not suggesting that this is a formal group. In fact as far as I know, none of the seven managers we've had in the past four and a half years have been aware of The Bunch's existence. It's just a group of individuals who are committed to each other, to the team as a whole, and to our customers. What I do know is that despite the lack of a consistent leader in a large global company going through a major company-wide reorganization, our group has grown from $5 million in revenue to $75 million in revenue. That's 667% growth (granted, starting from a small number).

Before I began writing this chapter I interviewed my teammates and asked them what they believed had allowed us to enjoy the success we've had, in spite of the headwinds we've faced. These were the common lessons learned:

First and foremost, it was the trust that we've formed between us. Much of that trust has come from the fact that we have gotten to know each other personally. We've bonded despite living in three different time zones, four different states, two different countries, and coming from four different generations.

When I asked the question, "Are we co-workers, or are we friends?" the answer I received most was, "Yes, I think we are both! Why can't we be? This shows up in very funny ways. For example, when I was asked during a call last Friday, "What are you doing this weekend?"

I responded, "Chris's mom and sister are coming over, and we are attending a play on Saturday."

Two teammates replied, "Tell PattyK and Shawna we said hello!"

Not only did they acknowledge both of them, but they knew their names without my telling them, and they had never met them, even on camera.

The few people who have left the company still attend the monthly after-hours meeting and are welcomed by all, and this close bonding makes it easy for the second lesson to happen.

The second lesson is that we bonded around a single purpose.

That purpose is to make every single individual within our team succeed. Within our group the words, "That is not my job," or, "That is not my account," are never heard.

We are salespeople being paid on commission, but if one of us needs help, every one of us steps in to do what we can to help—even though we know we won't get paid for that help. If you know anything about salespeople, you will understand how rare that is.

It may sound trite, but it really is all for one and one for all.

And finally we all feel free to be real with each other. We say, "I don't know," or "I screwed up," when it's appropriate.

The best part about all this is that it's contagious. The groups we work closest with have begun acting the same way. We're as open with them as we are with each other, and they have begun to reciprocate.

Together we work as one team. We support each other and it shows. We all have similar goals: to make each other succeed, to help each other grow, to support each other, and to make our customers happy.

For example, a few weeks ago a very small deal with a customer that we probably won't close came up. I was terribly busy with several large deals, as this was the fourth quarter of our fiscal year, when a great deal of pressure is on us. That small deal fell off my plate and I forgot about it.

The day before the presentation, the Account Executive called and asked me if I was ready to present. I told him I would be and hung up the phone. Immediately I called the director of the technical team that I work with, admitted my screw-up, and asked for help. He assigned the right people without hesitating and I was ready on time for the customer meeting the next day.

That wouldn't have happened four and a half years ago. Four and a half years ago I would have gotten a response more along the lines of, "It's not our fault you screwed up and didn't work this deal properly. We cannot be catering to unreasonable timeframes. You need to be better at your job so that we can do ours." And my customer would have suffered.

But not today. Today, our team and the teams that we touch

show caring and respect for each other. Because of that we're able to remove friction from our working lives and provide much better service to our customers, which, in the end, is all that matters.

We are doing our part to change a very large organization from inside our little part of the world.

Where there was once brown grass, green grass is now growing.

Brian Fippinger

With over 45 years of business experience, much of it in leadership roles at Global 500 companies, **Brian Fippinger** brings first-hand knowledge of what it takes to lead organizations and teams through turbulent times. As a coach, speaker, and facilitator, he integrates these experiences with his training in somatic-based learning, promise-based management, and improvisation to create a unique learning approach for his clients. Brian lives in Chicago with his wife Chris.

TEN

Purposeful Connection: From Courage to Possibility

Emily Raeker

I opened my email to yet another organizational change announcement. Managers, peers, projects and organizations shifted so frequently that it had become just another day on the job. I almost scrolled on by, but this particular announcement caught my attention. After almost a decade of this team being run by the all-male founders, my heart soared as I saw the announcement that a woman named Catherine would be our next corporate vice president.

At the time, Catherine and I had four layers of management between us. She had a phenomenal reputation and tremendous success at Microsoft. I knew she was human, just like me. And while she was given an amazing role, I imagined myself in her situation. She was stepping into Bob's shoes at the helm of the organization knowing that his leadership team were all men aside from his chief of staff.

While the team culture proclaimed to be flexible and growth-minded, after several years on the team I was well aware that the leaders had some blind spots when it came to culture and employee experience. The founders had done an amazing job, but it was time to bring us into the next phase of success.

As I considered this new leader, something told me I had to get to know her. Now—in my experience—most people are hesitant to reach out to higher up managers. I am a bit of an anomaly in that area.

"We all put our pants on the same way," I used to say to Josh, my previous manager. He and I worked together when I represented the National Institutes of Health and the US Department of Veterans Affairs. My mindset—seeing all people as humans and equals—often gave him a chuckle. I wondered if he was in awe of my courage—or perhaps befuddled by the success that this innocence (or perhaps ignorance) had led to in my career. Either way, that mindset *usually* served me well. I always respect the human and their role, but nerves rarely take over even when the top scientist or chief information officer of the world's highest healthcare offices demanded answers or made the rest of the team shudder. To me, they were human beings who needed answers and support. And I could deliver.

Knowing that we had an upcoming offsite in Seattle, I reached out to Catherine on Teams.

"Hi Catherine!" *Nope, too informal.*

"Good afternoon, Catherine!" *Nope. Where is my ask?* Gotta have an ask when reaching out to my corporate vice president. Admittedly, the gremlins in my mind were running amok.

Finally, "Welcome to the team, Catherine! I am excited to meet you and learn from you. Would you be open to connecting with me in Seattle? I plan to arrive early and would love to learn more about you!" *Send.*

Then those three little dots showed up. "..." A quick response! Having access to someone at that level can be an honor. Their days are packed and generally someone else handles communications for them. I was naturally thrilled at her willingness to engage directly and so quickly!

"Thank you for the warm welcome, Emily! Please reach out to my chief of staff to schedule 30 minutes. I look forward to meeting you," she replied.

Truth be told, I had no intention of traveling early. And I knew I

Purposeful Connection: From Courage to Possibility

would likely have to pay for the extra day in the hotel. But that little spark in my gut told me to do just that, and I listened to it.

The day comes. I bring my best Kate Spade bag, wear my favorite subdued rose gold jewelry, and confidently approach the conference room. I had thoroughly prepared for this meeting by looking at her LinkedIn account, thinking through my intro, preparing questions to ask her, deciding what stories I should share to earn her respect, and more.

We spent the entire half hour with me rambling on about myself. I learned nothing about her and came away upset with myself for wasting the opportunity to truly connect. I must admit, this meeting felt like it was one of the bigger failures of my career.

That evening as I reflected, it occurred to me that I did not ask her a single question even though my entire goal was to learn about her. I wondered how she got to where she is today? What was her path? What inspires her? How does she define success? How can I help her be successful? *What on earth was I thinking?!?*

So I open my laptop, click into Teams and type.

"Catherine, thank you for taking the time to connect today. My intention was to get to know you, and instead I talked about myself the entire time. I recognize you have a busy schedule. Would you be open to a do-over while I am in town? I would love to learn about your career, your vision for the team, and how you are doing in your new role. It is exciting to have a strong female leader, and I would love to learn from you. Thank you in advance for your consideration."

At the time I saw this act as tucking my tail and recouping from a big mistake. I did not appreciate the courage and humility it took for me to send her this message. Today I recognize that my follow-up was probably a big part of earning her respect.

I was shocked when Catherine accepted my request. She had a full schedule and asked if she could ping me when she had a break. The next business day goes by and not a word. I was so embarrassed, but I believed she would keep her word. I tucked my tail a bit and strolled back to my hotel as meetings came to an end. I fell back onto the hotel bed for some breathing exercises to clear my head, when suddenly I heard the sweet ding of a Teams notification.

"Emily, I'm sorry. The day has been so busy. I have time now. Are you still available?"

"Hi Catherine! Yes, of course. I will be there in eight minutes," I responded while quickly calculating the walk.

This time I found my inner curiosity and opened my mind. I saw interesting things in her office and asked about them. I asked about her stories and what it was like being a woman in this business. I asked how she felt about our organization and what she envisioned for our future. An hour and a half went by and we were still chatting. I was no longer trying to impress her. Instead I was having a blast getting to know her. She taught me the true definition of sponsorship and embodied the practice of lifting others up.

The next day our team had a social event. Catherine and I connected when she walked in, and she asked me to introduce her to a few people. I was able to reciprocate her sponsorship and generosity. Seeing this, my peers came up to me and eagerly asked me to introduce them to her!

While I did not appreciate why my gut told me to connect with her years ago, today I know confidently that connecting with her has been so important in my life. She gave me opportunities to lead and shine by appointing me as the inclusion lead for a massive organization. She helped me through big lessons and challenges. She sponsored me during awards discussions acknowledging the long-term impacts on my career. And when my heart guided me to follow a new path, Catherine emphatically supported me. I felt awful for vacating the incredible role to which I had been appointed. But she would have none of that. She was thrilled knowing that I could bring so much to the world with my new ideas while finding fulfilment.

Not only did she support my transition, she also introduced me to two amazing human beings. One was her neighbor, Sheila—my unbelievable coach—who has helped me find my own inner greatness in uncharted territory. Another was her sister's friend who is a meditation genius and tremendous photographer. Both of these women have had a huge impact on my life and my journey as well! Fast forward a few years, and she still serves as a sponsor, mentor, and now also a friend.

The winding path of connection

These experiences cannot be contained in a silo. My connection with Catherine would not have been possible had it not been for Scott who served as the executive sponsor during an intense customer escalation in 2018. He witnessed me in action and offered to be a mentor. Scott's mentorship and sponsorship led to my promotion, financial recognition, and progression into my next position. He also became a friend after retiring. He looked out for me when I experienced my first hurricanes living alone on the coast and introduced me to some amazing friends. His wife even guided me as I dipped my toes into the world of writing.

Meeting Scott would not have been possible had it not been for Josh betting on me to join his team in 2017 and subsequently giving me the opportunity to shine during several high profile customer escalations.

Meeting Josh would not have been possible had it not been for sitting next to Sean in the office, who became my confidant. We shared many laughs when I delivered a Microsoft social engagement training to a customer. Once, when I experienced intense harassment, Sean was there to lift me up and help me find resources and strength.

These types of connections go on and on. They apply to personal life with neighbors, friends, and people who welcomed me to a new town after I lost so much. So many stories, but only one chapter.

Paying it forward

When people ask me about my most memorable experiences or

impactful moments in my career, I always think of two situations where I lifted others up.

One was an engineer who was deflated, frustrated, annoyed, angry and completely resistant to me joining a project. After our time partnering on that project he quickly earned a gold club award and was promoted to principal. He shared with me that by investing in him, he learned to invest in others. And now he pays it forward.

Another was an incredible contractor on my team. He was eager, willing, had a phenomenal outlook, was proactive and always happy to deliver. I saw potential in him and knew he would be amazing as a full-time employee. I served as a sponsor for him to join Microsoft full-time, and within his first year of employment he also won a gold club award and was promoted to principal. On top of that, he serves as a beacon of light to the compliance space across the customer, partner, and employee base.

Since I started to write this chapter, I have connected with several other people from my past who shared my impact on them. One recently shared that four years later he still has saved tabs from things he learned working with me.

The courage to connect

Networking is a word that makes many of us uncomfortable. We are groomed in business to think it requires having a prepared request and an offer to the other person in return. Being courageous and purposeful with open curiosity can be drastically more powerful than networking in the formal sense of the word.

When those little nudges happen in your mind and your gut, take a chance. Reach out. Build a connection. By listening to these signs, you will be surprised. It will lead to personal and professional resilience, layoff resilience, new experiences and opportunities, and community in times of need. It will deliver an opportunity for you to lift others up and see them shine.

Where do you begin?

1. Find a few minutes all to yourself. Ground yourself in the moment. Take a few deep breaths in, and long slow breaths out. Reflect upon what spark or idea may be sitting in the back of your mind or felt in your gut. Have you been ignoring it or making excuses not to listen to it? Just being aware of what your heart, mind, gut, or intuition is saying is a huge first step.
2. Challenge yourself to notice when you hear that nudge. Simply notice.
3. Now, take action! A wave, a hello, a smile, a question. Reach out and connect with no specific intention in mind. Be open to what it may bring. And when that first meeting happens, simply celebrate the beginning.

As time unfolds, you will discover amazing possibilities arising from those tiny little actions. Embrace that excitement. Life may just amaze you!

Emily Raeker

Emily Raeker, Chief Inspiration Officer, utilizes mindfulness and self-compassion in her work with the Invictus Games Foundation, Beaufort Historical Association, and Soundscape Communities to deliver transformational people-focused and accessible experiences. Her Microsoft career was spent delivering global program successes for M365 products, enabling innovation for health and federal civilian clients, and leading efforts towards the continual growth of a trusting and inclusive culture. A Midwesterner by birth, Emily is at home by the ocean.

Disrupting Disconnection

Whatever affects one directly, affects all indirectly. I can never be what I ought to be until you are what you ought to be.

Martin Luther King, Jr.

ELEVEN

Humans Being Well

Niya Bajaj

"If you can't handle being here, you should consider working somewhere else."

I should have taken a sick day when I woke up with sensory overwhelm. The radiating pain from my clenched jaw felt like hot needles stabbing the back of my eyes. Instead, I logged in to a virtual meeting 30 minutes before my workday started because my manager urgently needed to talk to me. I was squinting at the overly bright screen and fumbling to find a volume setting that I could tolerate after another night of terrible sleep when she dropped that bomb. My face froze in a confused expression when she clarified by listing examples of how I seemed distracted in meetings, and not immediately responsive to her every request.

On a good day, I would have been able to tell her that my distraction came from a team culture that encouraged side-conversations in meetings. I would have shared that the six hundred emails a day, many from her with step-by-step instructions about how to send other emails, made it challenging to focus on conversations while attending to her urgent requests.

This was not a good day.

I sat there, dumbfounded, as the silence became awkward and

my palms and underarms turned slick with nervous sweat. As a Type-A, high achieving, award winning professional who has a long history of exceeding requirements and leading teams to do the same, I couldn't muster a single word in my defense. I was not sure I wanted to.

It had been six months since the world went into lockdown in response to COVID-19. Being stripped of my ability to make decisions about my life triggered a relapse of my eating disorder. My anorectic tendencies manifested as making and eating a single incredibly artistic charcuterie board a day. The pretty boards made me Instagram popular, encouraging my laser focus on perfecting them to gain more social capital. When everyone was struggling to maintain relationships it felt like a great way to stay connected without requiring emotional depth or honesty. At under a thousand calories, the boards were taking a nutritional toll, impeding my ability to think clearly and to manage my chronic pain condition. While my mental health struggle was difficult, it did not seem like a real problem relative to the suffering in the world. I was privileged to live in my own home, to be able to afford food, to be employed. I was not grieving the loss of parents or pregnancies like other women I knew. It seemed selfish to draw attention to my struggle and to use health-care resources when people were dying, so I kept it under wraps. I chose to share only the brightest, happiest parts of my life to inspire others with beauty, awe, and cat photos, because we all needed more of that.

This became especially important after George Floyd was murdered. At work I was assigned to support our executive lead on the new Anti-Black Racism taskforce to develop policy and procedure for our organization. As a woman with East Indian heritage, I had a personal interest in the work as an ally. I have lived expertise in how institutional racism and race-based workplace harassment compromise engagement, productivity, career advancement and irreparably harm health and well-being. In a volatile, uncertain, complex, and increasingly ambiguous environment, I found purpose in supporting my Black colleagues through strategizing around policy development. I was happy to use my privilege to raise questions about whether asking Black employees to share their experiences of workplace harassment was necessary or re-traumatizing, since we had decades of data to draw from. I was also happy to do the emotional labor of meeting one-on-one with the executive leads to encourage them to take a stronger stand and support the actions identified by the working groups.

Maintaining the performance of wellness while I collaborated on developing frameworks and held people to accountability standards worked, even as the secret-keeping about my declining mental health and increasing exhaustion impacted how present I was. After months of dedicated focus, I was invited into a one-on-one meeting with the executive lead and told that the project was being terminated. The organization had decided to go in a different direction, despite promises made that this was not going to be an empty exercise. I tried not to let my disappointment show. I was sad that I did not have the energy to be angry as I felt my deep sense of purpose fizzle out and become cynicism. What was the point of devoting my energy to an organization that didn't align with my values?

As the enforced social isolation continued, team members moved on to other jobs, and loneliness and languishing became silent companions. It became easier to decline invitations to eat virtual lunches together by citing a distaste for eating on camera to hide the fact that I wasn't eating. The disconnect from purposeful work, and the growing sense of distrust in leadership promises that the organization cared about well-being while they sent 11:00 p.m. emails, made it easy to opt out of morale-building activities. Feeling disconnected from the team and aware that much of the work I was doing did not align with my values led to that shocking morning meeting with my manager. It made me wonder if quitting was the right choice.

While pondering the decision, an invitation popped into my inbox. "Join us On the Stoop," it read. It was from one of my taskforce colleagues. When I dug for details I saw several familiar names on the list—all colleagues with systemically excluded identity markers who were also disappointed by the organizational decision. I accepted the invitation because I did not want to lose my tenuous link to these human beings. I wanted to stay connected to these courageous people who showed up as themselves, shared vulnerably about their challenging experiences, and wanted the same things I did—*healthy leaders leading healthier teams to deliver sustainable human-centered solutions rooted in equity and justice.*

That first meeting was eye-opening. It began with a deeply thoughtful, collaboratively delivered acknowledgement of the land —something that had become a performative act of lip-service in the organization. Instead of an awkward rote rehearsal of generic phrases in a prepared script I heard a deep connection to the land and a recognition of reciprocal relationship. Then, like a gathering that would happen with neighbours sitting on a stoop, conversation started flowing. Community members shared experiences of struggle with the system, of trying to balance homeschooling and caregiving while being expected to meet unreasonable deadlines without enough information. I was tempted to offer resources and solutions, but after mindfully pausing, I noticed that no one else was. Instead, they were listening deeply, reflecting, and occasionally sharing similar experiences. It made sense to see if I could listen too, instead of diving in with solutions to prove how helpful and worthy I was. The longer I observed, the more I noticed how every person present was holding space for the sharing. Comments in the chat were echoing and empathizing from a place of deep self-awareness.

It was difficult to quiet my inner "fixer" but as I leaned into being mindful and stayed present, I witnessed the practice of emotional intelligence beyond the buzzword that gets thrown around at leadership tables. I practiced self-regulation as colleagues shared their experiences of suffering through management decisions that failed to take humanity into account, so I could offer supportive co-regulation.

As the meeting progressed, I watched as this group of humans showed up as their whole selves because they felt they belonged. The virtual Stoop had space for all of us to arrive as we were, and to share hard things. The response from community included reflective sharing of similar experiences, and invitations to continue the conversation one-on-one, reducing the feeling of isolation with space to diffuse the emotional impact of the challenge.

As I attended more meetings, I built my sense of confidence in participating. I learned to share my reflective experiences because I had heard how beneficial storytellers found it when they knew they had empathetic listeners. Over time, I started sharing my story, to find the meaning in what seemed like meaningless struggle. The community generously made space for me to do so, without judgement or leaping to solution-sharing to fix an experience that I had not defined as a problem.

In those conversations, I felt seen, heard, and deeply listened to, for the first time in a long time. By setting clear guidelines, always establishing a community agreement to create a braver space, and modelling narrative competence, this virtual community knew more about my day-to-day experiences than my partner or my family, because they made it safe to share. I felt connected with others who were grappling with their mental well-being. I saw similarities with people who were questioning the purpose and values alignment with their work. I experienced the empathy of other exhausted folx teetering on the edge of burnout.

The Stoop was a place to share every aspect of life. While many of us were struggling, we were also sharing moments of joy. Pregnancies were announced, and the group commissioned me to make a blanket for an expected baby because I was always crocheting in meetings. We celebrated when members left toxic teams for new opportunities. We congratulated members who successfully managed to host their COVID weddings. We also stood by each other in difficult times, sending flowers when loved ones passed.

This is the community who rallied around me when my cat died, because they had seen her in meetings. My immediate work team did not. It is the same community that encouraged organizational change by scheduling meetings with senior leaders to propose updates to corporate communications processes to better support employees grappling with significant uncertainty and wondering if their leaders saw their suffering. It is the community that offers an open invitation to anyone who wants to gather, share, seek support or offer it as we grapple with major world events. It is also the community that restores my sense of purpose, and that helped me bounce back from burnout. Every member of the group leans into critical leadership behaviours and supports each other in practicing emotional intelligence, accountability, narrative competence, and a deliberate focus on generative conflict where it's okay to be wrong and change your mind. This ensures that we go beyond the inclusion level of psychological safety, all the way to challenger safety. This committed practice is what grounds the strong social connections that make it safe to show up in a conversation and share the reality of suffering and struggle that is being human. It is what inspires connection to a community that restores a sense of purpose rooted in shared values of kindness, presence, and an active offer of support. It is what makes it okay to raise questions about how we can better support each other by centering our social well-being through meaningful relationships where each of us is of service to each other.

How will you create your Stoop? Here is the ABC and S that make it possible for people to feel like they belong, form lasting friendships, reduce languishing and loneliness, and create a wellness-centered culture where everyone can flourish.

Act with purpose

The personal invitation I received was a clear indication that my presence was desired. The warm welcome from the community confirmed that my membership and participation as an active listener were valued. These purposeful actions encouraged my engagement in a time of overwhelm. With a community of hundreds, it can be difficult to stay true to a mission. On The Stoop succeeds at being a welcoming, engaging community because everyone's actions—from choosing speakers to scheduling meetings to setting agendas—is rooted in a clear, collaborative sense of purpose. This deep connection reduces the churn of tasks generated to meet the need for performance optics, which helps mitigate the chronic stress and loss of personal efficacy that contributes to burnout.

Be human with humans

Vulnerability is challenging, especially in the workplace, where self-stigma and cultural stigma add barriers to being our whole selves. Leaning in to sharing your lived expertise makes it safer for others to do the same and supports a sense of belonging, which is the basis of psychological safety. Observing my peers practice bravery and share their truest thoughts and experiences made it safer for me to find my courage, participate in dialogue, engage in community building, and eventually establish the trust that grounds my friendships. That trust is what makes it safer for me to test new ideas and ways of being, including setting and sticking with boundaries, in community. It also creates an atmosphere where I can pose divergent ideas and we can conduct thought experiments about changes to our culture. If the Stoop did not include a commitment to open, honest conversation, where we take risks and explore new ways of being, we would all still be loosely affiliated colleagues instead of closely knit friends.

Center being well

In addition to building a sense of comfort and belonging, The Stoop is a place where caring for each other's well-being is central to everything we do. This focus on well-being, across all eight aspects (physical, mental, emotional, spiritual, social, environmental, financial, and occupational) shows up in how we support each other. My favorite way to extend this care is through leading nervous system regulation practices that support physical and emotional well-being for the community. Other members offer practice interviews or job application reviews to support occupational and financial well-being. Others plan learning events to support mental and social well-being. Each of us brings something to the table in our personal and larger group relationships that deepens our sense of trust and connection with each other. Centering well-being in this way also makes room to share struggles and to ask for help, instead of masking and pretending perfection.

Share stories

A lot of On The Stoop's success is grounded in a shared practice of narrative competence—the ability to listen deeply, recognize the embodied impact, understand the storyteller's verbal, tonal, and nonverbal communication, make meaning from story, and take values-aligned action. This requires a willingness to be vulnerable in sharing and receiving stories—which I received when I was finally brave enough to share my stories with the group. Their deep listening created a soft landing space where I could reflect on what I was going through. I heard it echoed in empathetic sentiments which reminded me that I was not alone in my experience. When I was ready to explore recovery, I asked for and received the gift of creative solutions to test in my experience. If that's not what friends are for, I don't know what is.

Your Stoop is out there, waiting for you to invite your community. My heart is full of hope for your success.

Niya Bajaj

Niya Bajaj, award winning mentor and Champion of Mental Health, is an internationally certified holistic yoga therapist and narrative medicine facilitator. She has coached over 500 people-leaders through the Mindfulness for Leaders program and delivers bespoke wellness-centered leadership learning experiences that support organizational culture change for improved employee well-being, engagement, and performance at organizations including Accenture, Brookfield Investments, Royal Bank of Canada, Bank of Montreal, and the University of Toronto.

TWELVE

Super-Connecting

Claire Wissler

"No, go ahead without me. I'm going to eat at my desk today." That was my standard response when asked to go to lunch with my coworkers. I was often operating under tight deadlines and trying to preserve a social life outside of work. A lunch break felt like a poor use of my time. While my coworkers took a leisurely break to chat and eat lunch in the California sunshine, I stayed at my desk. *I can get more work done if I don't join them*, I reasoned.

Growing up, I was always a good student. Quiet in class. Turned in my homework on time. Active participant in group projects. This strategy paid off—I got straight As and praise from my teachers. School, in short, had a singular purpose: get good grades so you can get a good job. I valued my friends, but they were relegated to the time after school and on weekends.

When I entered the workforce in my twenties, I expected to be as successful at work as I had been in school. I determined that *success* was sitting in the corner office, and to get there required doing good work so that I could get promoted. I set my sights on climbing the corporate ladder and friends, once again, were relegated to nights and weekends.

I learned quickly that the primary measurement of *good work* is a glowing performance review. Twice a year I would receive ratings on the competencies I was expected to display: flawless execution; focus; clear communication; reliability; judgement; and leadership. Channeling my inner over-achiever, I reasoned that while it was good for my coworkers to see these qualities in my work, it would be even better for them to believe I operated my personal life like this as well. I was supposed to be buttoned-up and put together.

I let my drive to be the perfect promotion candidate direct my social interactions at the office. I didn't want to be seen eating lunch with a crowd of interns. Would associating with the interns make management think I was immature?

I certainly didn't tell my manager when I was struggling with a breakup or stressed about a sick family member. Would showing emotions make them doubt my ability to lead the next big project?

Once I became a manager, the same rules applied. When a member of my team asked what I did over the weekend, the answer was always the same. "Oh, nothing much. It was a quiet weekend." I didn't want to risk sharing details about my personal life that could cause the team to question my authority.

Above all I took the competency of *focus* the most seriously. I didn't prioritize remembering the name of a coworker's husband or where they were going on their next vacation. I thought it better to reserve that brain power for memorizing Q4 budget numbers and ensuring I had put together a tight agenda for the next meeting.

I valued praise from coworkers on my job skills. It felt so affirming to hear coworkers say, "Claire is quick at responding to requests," or, "she's a creative problem-solver." Having a singular goal of climbing the corporate ladder wasn't always enjoyable but it generally worked. I leveraged positive performance reviews to get a promotion. Then I leveraged that promotion to get a more prestigious job at a bigger company. I repeated this process again and again as my resume continued to shine.

To maintain the illusion of perfection at work, I hid my true self behind a pleasant but not overly friendly shell. I thought that creating barriers between my work and personal life protected me

Super-Connecting

from criticism at the office. And in some ways, it did. Yet I was also starving myself from the exact thing I needed when things got hard—genuine human connection.

Last year, I got the news that my department was being restructured and my position would be eliminated. My seemingly perfect career was shattered in a single phone call. As the dust settled from the initial shock, I came to realize what I was left with when my employment ended. Once I was locked out of my laptop, eight years of artifacts from my work efforts disappeared in an instant. All the documents, emails, and reports that I spent so much time on were reduced to bits and bytes in the Cloud that would likely never be looked at again. And that promotion I bent over backwards to get suddenly felt hollow and meaningless—reduced to a line on my résumé.

Not only did I lose access to my work files, but my abrupt departure from the team severed communication with most of my former coworkers. My office conversations primarily centered around an urgent request for a report or preparing for an upcoming presentation. When my work ties were cut, my former coworkers and I had nothing else in common and no other reason to connect. My protective shell had seen to that.

Without the structure of a full-time job, I started reflecting on how I wanted to fill my newly found free time. Not one day went by where I missed the pressure of executive meetings or nitpicking bullet points in a slide deck. What I did find is that I was craving social connections to help process my period of transition.

Several months earlier, I had enrolled in a course on conscious leadership and authentic communication, but I hadn't made time to attend the lectures due to my busy work schedule. Now, I joined every session I could, learning how to build relationships in new ways, making genuine connections with people of varying ages, backgrounds, and abilities. Without the crutch of work as a topic of conversation, I was forced to dig deeper into my authentic self for things to say. I found that people were responsive to my vulnerability by being vulnerable in return. I was beginning to see the stark contrast between the new relationships I was building, and the surface-level interactions I had with my coworkers.

In hindsight, I can see how much I used to hide in my shell at the office. How calculated I was about sharing personal information or socializing, and how much I missed out on as a result. I knew I worked with talented people, but I didn't really *know* most of them. And they certainly didn't know me. Frankly, I didn't even know myself. I have learned that it is through open-hearted relationships with a diverse group of people that we gain larger perspectives on life. Often we come to understand ourselves better in the process too.

Looking back on my career I can see examples of people who operated differently than I did. I remember one coworker in particular who had the positivity and patience to pierce my professional shell. I've given a lot of thought to the lessons I can learn from him.

"Hey Claire, we're going to lunch. Do you want to come?" my new co-worker Ara asked years earlier.

Oh boy. What do I say? I thought to myself, staring back at this smart, energetic, junior-level employee. I paused, the usual questions circling around in my head. *Did I want to be seen eating lunch with someone junior to me? What would management think? That I wasn't qualified to get promoted? Or I wasn't professional enough?* But there was something about Ara's bright personality that melted a bit of my cold exterior. I quieted that part of me that was afraid of appearances, and I accepted.

Over the course of the two years I worked with Ara, it became clear to me that his ability to connect on a personal level applied to coworkers of all kinds. He didn't shy away from being social and had relationships with people in every department of the company. He also had a kind persistence that I appreciated—I could say no to lunch invitations five times in a row, yet he would continue to stop by my desk and ask. He didn't just convince me to carve out the occasional 30 minutes for a lunch break. I found myself dropping my walls and showing some of my true self when I spent time with Ara.

Ara was able to achieve his professional goals without sacrificing social connection and experiences with his coworkers. People like him bring social magic to a team. They are super-connectors who can relate to diverse personalities and hold conversations that don't include, "Can you get that to me by end of day?" As extroverts, they thrive on social connection. It's effortless for them to organize a happy hour or introduce a new team member to others in the organization.

Super-connectors also create a sense of safety for employees who find themselves trying to keep up appearances with management. Often being an individual contributor, honest conversations with them have fewer implications on performance reviews or compensation decisions. They create something akin to a mycelium network below the surface of a team, providing nutrients in the form of a coffee break or lunchtime chat to those who might need a little bit of extra motivation, or simply a break from the day-to-day grind.

Are you a super-connector? Lean in! You are an invaluable part of your team culture. You are often connecting people like me who need a little nudge to get away from their desk for a bit.

Do you manage a super-connector? Find ways to support and reward their efforts. They are playing a role that you can't play on the team. The time they spend organizing happy hours or chatting casually with co-workers pays long-term dividends towards building a positive team culture.

Are you an introvert? Seek out the super-connectors on your team. You might feel an aversion to striking up conversations with strangers, but this is likely effortless for a super-connector. Let them do some of the leg work for you. Go to the happy hour or the offsite lunch they are organizing. Connecting with other people on a personal level at work might feel like more effort than it's worth—but I've learned that it is incredibly important.

I regret that I didn't prioritize the development of deeper relationships with my coworkers. Keeping people at arm's length felt safe, but human connection is the antidote to feeling unsafe. A pristine project plan is a poor source of comfort in a tumultuous work environment.

I will also be redefining *success* in my future roles. While a singular focus on career advancement may work for some, I ultimately found it unfulfilling and lonely. I don't need to treat my job the way I treated school—having the singular purpose of building credentials for the next step. There is potential to have a much richer experience at work. One that not only satisfies my desire for achievement but also meets the need for social connection, learning, and growth.

Although I have cultivated new skills for building authentic relationships, I recognize I'm still an introvert at heart. So, I'll be seeking out those super-connectors in my next role and leaning on them as I work to integrate myself into the social thread of an organization. I want the next phase of my career to involve more than just spreadsheets. I want to take advantage of the opportunity to connect to the wonderful people I'm working with and make a conscious effort to get to know them. When I leave my next job, I want to have built something I can take with me—real connections that are not subject to any work contract.

And above all, I want to eat more lunches in the sunshine.

Claire Wissler

Claire Wissler believes that authentic communication with others is a path to deeper self-understanding. She has extensive experience in marketing analytics across the retail and technology industries. She enjoys hiking through the tranquility of nature, experiencing new cultures through travel, and searching vintage shops for mid-century pieces for her home.

THIRTEEN

A Mystery Solved

Nicole Ennen

Was I in a sitcom?

I approached the venue with a mix of excitement and trepidation. I just started a new job and I was about to meet my coworkers for the first time.

But I was not outside of the office. I was about to walk into a murder mystery party.

The organization had a team-building event scheduled the week before my official first day and invited me to attend. I took this invitation, and the fact that the company was investing in team-building events, as a great sign, starting to build my expectations of the work culture. As I stepped through the door, I prepared myself for the comedic events about to unfold. During the interview process, I had only met the leadership team virtually and they were not in attendance. In addition to the murder, I had another mystery to solve—figure out who was a colleague and who was an actor in the play.

Navigating the evening proved an interesting challenge.

"What character are you again?" I was asked by a colleague.

"Actually, I'm the new manager—starting Monday," I replied.

Awkward laughs and introductions followed. I felt slightly

accomplished that I mistook others less than they mistook me. We were split into tables and served dinner, allowing me to learn more details about a few of my new coworkers. By the end of the night my table had not solved the murder but I did end up determining who was an actor. I enjoyed getting introduced to my new colleagues in an informal setting, and was excited to start working with them.

My assumption based on the party was that the team culture was open, fun, and relaxed. I came to quickly understand that this was not the case. Upon my arrival in the office, I realized the play we just attended was a lot more structured than our work. There was not a clear onboarding process or any clear documentation on everyone's roles and responsibilities. Throughout my first week, I recognized that I had many more mysteries to tackle. *Where did I fit in relation to my coworkers? Who was actually responsible for different decisions? What were the organization's priorities?* As I would come to find out, these were a lot harder to solve than the murder.

Over the first few weeks, my colleagues did not appear to be as open with sharing their thoughts and feelings as I had anticipated. Our off-site leadership struggled to communicate clear priorities, which often caused confusion and dissension. There was a lot of pressure to move quickly to meet our client deliverables, leaving little time for us to get to know one another. The environment was not set up for us to have an open and honest dialogue. Small miscommunications turned into larger issues, slowing down productivity. Everyone was moving too fast to actively listen. What happened to my fellow detectives who were so open to sharing clues?

I have always loved learning about other people's personalities, hearing their stories, and truly getting to know what makes them tick. Yet, I found myself holding back from building bonds in this office, keeping communication surface level. That kind of behavior did not seem to be accepted.

Because of this environment, many of us fundamentally did not understand one another.

"Why are you moving forward without my approval on this?"

my peer office manager asked during one of our conflicts over scope and responsibilities.

Due to the lack of role clarity, we would sometimes duplicate work or debate who owned which decisions. Recognizing that instances like this not only caused tension, but also slowed down our productivity, I finally convinced our leaders that we needed to invest time in learning each other's communication and work styles.

Finally, some clues were revealed. That colleague and I had vastly different approaches to work. I liked action. I got enough information and then moved forward quickly. She liked to research and wanted all of the options before making a decision. After this understanding, we worked much better together, compromising on what was enough information to act. If only it happened sooner, we would have saved ourselves a year of frustration.

I came to realize that an underlying cause of how colleagues interacted were the behaviors of the virtual executive leadership team. Priorities changed constantly throughout my tenure, keeping everyone on edge. Decisions were made in silo without input from those of us in the office. Secrets were kept, and only shared when it benefited them. It was like playing the boardgame Clue, but instead of not knowing the murder weapon, room, or perpetrator, we did not know key information to be effective in our roles. Executives kept those cards close to their chests. Over time it escalated not quite to murder, but to toxic layoffs. At one point, I was explicitly told to lie to my direct manager. I was invited to a leadership retreat, but she was not. The company was going through a round of downsizing and they were trying to cut my manager out. Fearing for my own position, I kept my mouth shut. To this day I regret not bringing that toxic behavior to light. Shortly after that incident, I started looking for another job.

The external "fun" events, like the murder mystery parties, fancy dinners, and even leadership retreats to tropical locations, became a shiny cover to hide the truth. The office was not a safe place to fully be myself. I locked away my personal life when I was at work, and only shared what was necessary. I did not trust the executive leaders and neither did my colleagues, leading to a culture of fear and hidden agendas. Luckily, after a couple months of job searching, I locked in a role at another company. I did not know it at the time, but this new team would help me crack the case on the components of a positive and effective team culture.

Clues shared, solutions discovered

"Can't wait to work with you!"
"Super excited that you will be joining the team!"
Emails like this rolled in right after I signed my acceptance letter. "Do you need information on what area to live in?" one colleague asked.

I had not met many of my new coworkers during the interview process, yet they were offering to help me find my place in the new city. It was not just the gesture, but that they genuinely seemed to care about me as a person. Before I was technically an employee, I already felt like a part of the team.

In my first week, I was assigned an onboarding buddy—a peer on my team who showed me around the office, introduced me to colleagues, and was available if I had any questions. Taking time to build relationships seemed not only accepted, but encouraged by leadership. There was a lot of work to be done yet my manager, my onboarding buddy, and my coworkers made time for me. A part of my onboarding plan was to meet with each of my teammates individually. We shared information about ourselves, I learned about their skillsets, and they helped me understand the team's processes. Clues on how the office worked came together quickly, giving me a clear understanding of everyone's roles and responsibilities.

My manager met with me often, sharing expectations and offering support, but also giving me autonomy in actually doing the work. I knew *what* I should be doing, and the *how* was up to me. Her support allowed me to be vulnerable and ask for help when I needed it. A few months in I came to her very self-conscious about sending a big update to our top leaders. Instead of doing it herself, she took the time to give me encouragement and feedback. I sent the update

A Mystery Solved

and it was received well. Because of the safety of the environment, I was able to take on new tasks and build skills that I would not have been able to elsewhere.

Due to the time spent building relationships, there was an underlying sense of trust and psychological safety that permeated throughout the team. We celebrated each other's success and we were there to help each other if we fell. At our team meetings every week, we had dedicated time to both recognize each other's accomplishments and ask for assistance. When we were faced with complex problems, we could brainstorm different viewpoints, and instead of it turning into conflict, we came up with better solutions. Because we had a shared level of understanding of one another, we were able to have difficult conversations.

"Can we grab coffee to discuss this project?" I asked my onboarding buddy about a year into my tenure on the team.

We were both working on a project and our scopes had started to overlap, causing duplication and process issues. Sound familiar? Once we recognized what was happening, we had an open conversation, making compromises and resolving the situation efficiently so it did not impact our productivity. Unlike my last role, no one on the team hid the evidence. Instead, we shared it so we could work better together.

One day, I had the realization that I was not only working with colleagues, but with friends. We discovered that we shared interests with one another outside of work. Some of us joined an intramural sports team together. One of our coworkers was an extra in a movie, so we all went to the theater. Some of us even took weekend trips together. I felt that my teammates were able to see me as a full person, and vice versa. They saw my quirks and oddities, but did not see me as less effective at work because of them. It was the opposite. Our understanding of one another led to better collaboration on our projects, helping us to consistently achieve or exceed our goals.

I did not appreciate this environment fully until it was gone. Over time, my career progressed and I moved on to new roles. Some of these new teams were much like the first—they had the external optics of big team-building events, fancy dinners, and expensive holiday parties, but something was missing. The small, daily behaviors that helped build effective relationships were not there. The environments where we could speak openly, felt supported, and were the most productive had a key element: we trusted one another.

Building a foundation of trust

Trust is a component that arises in many of the models on what makes effective teams.[1] It is found not only to be important for employee satisfaction, but also for productivity—teams and organizations with higher levels of trust perform better.[2] My former high-trust team was the most productive environment I have ever worked in. Not only did we achieve our team objectives, but we as individuals were rewarded for it—many of us experiencing promotions within a couple of years. That first company where no one trusted the executives nor each other is no longer in business. The lack of relationships and trust caused vast issues with productivity, eventually leading to closure. Work gets done by people, through people. Without trusting relationships, accomplishing anything is an uphill battle.

So, if trust is essential, how do we build it? For starters, mysteries are fun, but not at work. As employees, we want to know what our role is and what is expected of us. We want to understand the team vision and objectives and how we fit into the bigger picture. We want open communication and honesty from our leadership so we understand what is going on. This lays the foundation for trust as it lets us know what to expect from our environment.

We also need opportunities, on a day-to-day basis, to get to know one another. It is not about the big off-sites, the expensive holiday parties, or the fancy dinners. Sure those can be tools for recognition, but they are not enough. They are icing on the cake, adding to the experience, but implemented alone they are rather useless. What really matters, what builds that trust between colleagues, are those everyday behaviors—meeting individually to understand each other's roles; asking genuinely how one another is doing; taking time to learn about each other's personalities, work styles, and interests; building in time during team meetings for recognition; helping and supporting one another when challenges arise. It is essential to set up our work environments and processes so employees have the space to do these activities. The little things go a long way.

Not all of us can solve a murder, but we can create an environment where trusting relationships grow and thrive at work.

Nicole Ennen

~

Nicole Ennen, Founder of Org Empathy Consulting, LLC, works with organizations to develop their leaders, build interpersonal skills in employees, and create positive team cultures. Combining her MA in I/O Psychology, certifications in Hogan Leadership Assessments, and over a decade of experience leading People Operations teams, she helps organizations balance the complexities of doing business and being human. Nicole currently lives in San Jose, California.

FOURTEEN

Good Morning, Ni Hao, Hola, Guten Morgen!

Hsiao-Tung Lo

"I made a comment yesterday that may have offended you, but it was not directed towards you."

I received this message one Friday afternoon after a very stressful interaction with a colleague. While she thought her words and reaction were too aggressive, I didn't feel the same way. It's probably because I grew up having relatively straightforward conversations and interactions. But I did want to have a casual chat with her to see whether everything was alright after the meeting.

"No worries, I understood the stress, and thanks for the clarification," I replied and immediately felt less tense. Realizing that there were no bad feelings between us, I was ready for a nice weekend.

Working as part of a team with diverse backgrounds has been a learning curve. Being a member of an international team for almost five years, I have noticed how we've adapted our behaviors in order to achieve better outcomes with each other. Clarifying what we say —and not just our intentions behind our sentences—has become a necessity due to the limitations of our English vocabularies.

"We must do things this way," one colleague stated when we were at a crucial point in a project. It seemed like a pretty strong and aggressive way to communicate. I got a weird feeling and asked someone else about how he worded the request.

"He doesn't mean *must*," my team member explained. "That's just the way his inner translation comes out in English words."

None of us want to be misunderstood or mean to hurt anyone; we all have good intentions. In this case, I was able to ask additional clarification questions, which helped me express my point of view more clearly for the benefit of the whole team. As time goes by, I see my team members feel more comfortable communicating in the workspace, learning to listen carefully and provide feedback and share thoughts based on their own unique backgrounds.

Over time I've learned to recognize the interplay between subconscious and conscious thinking and sharing in different contexts. Being open to understanding makes meaningful differences in the workspace. The feeling of being remembered and cared for is powerful.

Born and raised in Taiwan, I have lived in the United States for around five years, transitioning from Master's student to full-time employee. I admit that this time was marked by endless nights thinking about why I was here, in a country far away from home, alone without any family members to support me.

The good news is, now I enjoy the person I have become and the work-life balance I have achieved. A majority of these results came from the experiences I gained at work that changed my mindset and supported me in deepening relationships in the workspace.

Embrace language diversity with patience and respect

"We are extending an offer to you," I remember hearing on a call a few weeks before my graduation.

The excitement lasted for about a week. I started worrying. *What if I cannot fit into the company culture? What if I cannot understand the meetings? What if I cannot answer the questions? What if others cannot understand what I am saying or what I want to express?*

It seemed hilarious to be nervous about my language skills even though I had a Master's degree and a good GPA, and did well in my presentations and group projects. But when I started that new job I was so nervous. I was the only Asian in a diverse team with colleagues from nine different countries. It is obvious we grew up speaking different languages. By default, the team uses English as a common language to communicate, which makes sense. This seems so easy and normal but we often forget that not everyone is a native English speaker nor equally proficient. For me, after listening to English sentences I translate them into Mandarin in my brain, prepare my response in Mandarin, process it into English, then speak up. Our team recognized that we were all trying our best to communicate. With this awareness, we became more patient, trying not to interrupt each other in the middle of conversations, waiting until each person finishes their sentences.

"Thanks for being patient in the meeting, I spoke slowly because my English is not good," I messaged a team member after a call.

"Ah no, you speak perfect English. Everyone can understand your point clearly," he responded. "You have good ideas, try to speak up more in the meetings in addition to typing the message."

Hearing this meant a lot to me and gave me more confidence. The first time I joined one of the company workshop events, everyone was asked to share one fun fact about themselves as an icebreaker, but no ideas popped up.

"You speak two different languages!" a colleague suggested. "I can only speak one."

In that moment I realized we all should be proud of ourselves instead of feeling ashamed of our accents or vocabulary or our relatively longer response times. Acknowledging that not everyone speaks the same languages, and creating a space without judgement in which speaking up is not only acceptable but desirable—is crucial.

Communication is not just about talking; it also includes listening.

As a Mandarin speaker my thought pattern is circular, while English speakers think in a mostly linear way. For example, I tend to say things like, "Remember the meeting last week? You supported me in my proposal, I am grateful for that." But a native English speaker would say, "I am grateful for your support in my proposal during the meeting last week."

Do you see the difference? In conversations with the China team, I need to be more patient and wait until they finish their reasoning before understanding the conclusion or result that they're imparting. Whereas when talking with US team members, I don't need to feel offended when they mention results or conclusions at the beginning of a conversation, because they will share the reasoning afterward.

Understanding different language backgrounds increases effective communication, reduces misunderstanding, and makes it even easier to build consensus within a team.

Stay curious about different cultural holidays

"Good morning, Ni Hao, Hola, Guten Morgen!" One day my manager started our daily stand-up meetings with greetings in different languages. This was such a warm welcome, and with only minor effort, that made everyone smile. A formal meeting doesn't need to start with serious ideas; bringing everyone's hearts together is what matters for a more effective discussion afterwards.

I have these kinds of conversations every year before I go on my one-week vacation for an important holiday in my culture.

"Happy Lunar New Year!"

I was surprised and impressed at the same time. "Thank you, that wasn't expected!"

Based in Denver, Colorado I follow the US calendar. It feels nice for the holiday to be cared about because none of my other colleagues are from Taiwan and they don't need to remember it.

I'm often asked, "What do you usually do to celebrate?" and I'm always glad to share.

Throughout the year our team chats about different holidays from different countries and cultures, which for us deepens connections in the workspace. It feels like we're not just here to work. We're being cared for and treated as humans, not just machines. Being asked about your opinion feels good and it makes people feel valuable. The workspace relationship doesn't need to be transactional all the time. Likewise, I do the same thing—embracing genuine curiosity to create connections with my colleagues.

I have also learned that when you become open within conversations, others do too. Opening up is a great way to motivate individuals to explain more, which further enhances understanding. When everyone is comfortable with sharing their opinions, the dynamic of the team transitions from collaborative to trusting.

Be aware of the limitations of different cultural events and restrictions

A diverse team can provide value in so many different ways other than just working on assigned tasks. Little things make a meaningful impact. From spending time learning about cultural norms and traditions, to finding a restaurant with a menu that accommodates every team member's different cultural dietary needs—simply letting the members know we are trying to consider everyone makes a difference.

There is certain period of the year when Colombia has repeated holidays on Mondays.

We sent out an email: "We would love for you to enjoy your holidays; do you need any support or should we reschedule some meetings?"

For the Colombian colleagues in our team, we didn't want to spoil important holidays in their culture, so we started thinking about what kind of ideas we could offer them.

If I haven't mentioned it before, I'm part of a fully-remote team. During our annual team in-person gathering, team members brought different sweet from their countries. We were able to try Colombian coffee, Taiwanese pineapple cake, Moroccan baklava, and Swedish pancakes. When we have a good team connection and cultural recognition, we realize we're not just co-workers. People naturally share their culture with those with whom they feel comfortable, and this is a feeling of natural friendship. We spend 40 hours a week working, more than half our waking time with colleagues. To maintain this long-term, it's critical to maintain our mental health and to feel that the work environment is suitable for us. Sometimes we need to slow down, make casual connections with the colleagues we meet every day and not always talk about formal stuff. This can invisibly build friendships in the workspace.

Encourage sharing personal stories

Genuine personal stories usually reduce the distance between colleagues more effectively than serious conversations. They show we care about each other as a human. Creating time and space to have open forums and share life experiences such as hometowns or even cultural shock within a diverse team, helps the team to get to know each other better. It's a starting point for conversations in other formal meetings and strengthens connections in the workspaces.

For my first year in the company I was part of the IT engagement team—also the year the entire department went remote due to the pandemic. During this challenging time, the team and I held a virtual event to engage the department globally: "What's Outside of Your Window." I gathered photos from associates and put them on the world map on a shared screen. From my hometown classic Taipei 101 to India's Taj Mahal, and from the Berlin Wall to Chile's Andes Mountain—it offered us broad insight into our cultures, values, and diverse offerings. Based on the engagement level and feedback shared afterwards, everyone enjoyed the event.

One day, a message popped up in my Teams.

"Can you share some good Asian markets near your location? My son-in-law is from Hong Kong and it would be helpful for him to consider if he wants to move here."

We had never worked together before but it felt nice to be

remembered for where I came from. This camaraderie was due to the virtual event where we could get to know each other better through the personal stories we were willing to share.

At work we often talk about effective communication or how to make better decisions—or the emerging topic of diversity and inclusion. But real workspace connection is not just about talking. It's also about reflecting different cultural understandings.

A diverse team should not be seen as an obstacle or something to avoid, but as a huge and distinct opportunity for better collaboration in the workplace and for the building of a company culture where every background is valued and recognized.

Hsiao-Tung Lo

∽

Hsiao-Tung Lo is a tech professional, speaker, author, and global ambassador for Women in Tech. She is committed to building a diverse and empathetic world in the workplace and passionate about empowering individuals to embrace their multidimensional potential and pursue the roles they aspire to. As a thought-leader and lifelong advocate for inclusivity, she actively works with international teams to demonstrate how diversity creates thriving and supportive environments.

FIFTEEN

The Broken Shield

Kevin Franzman

My hands were shaking. There was a quiver in my voice. I hated these unconscious reactions undermining my resolve, but I wasn't going to back down. We weren't just coworkers, we were friends and this decision wasn't right.

But can you be friends with your coworkers, truly? You can enjoy tackling tasks together. You can make jokes and share interests. You can complement each other on your achievements and console each other about your hardships. But does that make you friends? Will you do what's right for each other even if it risks your position? Can you maintain your friendship at different levels in the org chart? Does the current state of the workplace really allow us to be friends?

I was a software engineering manager overseeing half a dozen engineers in a remote work environment. My direct reports were those high performing team players that you hope to be blessed with as a manager. I also had a great relationship with my own boss. We had both started as engineers and spent time as managers together before he was promoted again. As my manager, he cared about my career development and job satisfaction. Even though he was my boss, we still made time during our meetings to laugh about a silly meme or discuss the video game we were playing that weekend. Things were going quite well.

Until they weren't.

A member of my team was struggling to get his task completed, which involved adding a new vendor for our meal delivery service. Delayed tasks were nothing out of the ordinary, but I checked in. I found that there were a variety of reasons for the delay, some outside his control, some within. The spec he received needed multiple rewrites. The meal delivery service was a complex system. The engineer had some struggles with his coding proficiency. I documented everything, met with the engineer, and we felt good about a path forward.

Then one day my boss called me up. I watched him in the Zoom window of my monitor in silence. His eyes were looking down, away from the camera. He removed his glasses and began fiddling with the distinctive red frames. He seemed nervous. Finally, he broke the silence: "You know the task to add a new vendor to meal delivery?"

"Oh, yeah. I know it's gotten a bit delayed, but I've chatted with the engineer and we've got a plan to get it moving again," I replied casually.

He didn't really seem interested in my answer. Instead, my boss just continued: "Well, somehow this task came on my bosses' radar. They asked who was assigned the task." He paused for a moment.

"Ok…" I said, unsure of where he was going with this.

He looked up at me with a determination in his eyes, like he had just made a decision. "They said Kevin needs to fire that engineer."

I was shocked. Upper management knew next to nothing about the employee or the situation. All they had was a high-level overview from our ticketing system. On the other hand, as his direct manager, I was the one who actually knew about his job performance. I had worked with him on many occasions, observed his interactions with the team, heard his updates during team stand ups and received good feedback about him from coworkers. Like anyone else, he had both strengths and weaknesses. While he struggled with some coding tasks, he excelled at teamwork, often being the first to volunteer to help others.

The Broken Shield

I also knew him as a person. His eyes would light up as he told me about his daughter starting preschool and he was passionate about the chickens he was raising. He enjoyed working alongside others and often filled our team collaboration sessions with his deep laugh.

I had documented his performance over his term on my team. I fairly included both his successes and his mistakes. I outlined everything that had gone on with the task, including how he stepped up to fix the spec by doing the work that should have been done by the product analyst.

How could termination, with no consultation, no chance for improvement, no warning, be their decision?

This went entirely against my beliefs. Companies should treat employees with respect when the employees show the company respect. Companies should have standard practices for performance improvement so everyone is treated fairly. Firing this hard-working, respectful team player with no chance to improve was unacceptable to me.

I was livid. The intense emotion was bubbling up inside me. I could hear the blood rushing in my ears. I could feel my hands begin to shake. Instead of a hot rage, I felt cold, like the anger was a black hole pulling the heat from my body. I did my best to maintain my composure and told my boss all these findings: the irregularities of the task, the engineer's performance, my beliefs.

My manager cautioned me that I should do what his bosses say or risk my own place at the company. But this engineer's well-being was my responsibility.

As his leader, this man was under my protection and I was determined to be his shield, whatever the cost.

So, I told my boss that if they insisted I fire him right then and there, I'd quit.

Silence overtook the call again. My boss's wide eyes told me that this was not the reaction he expected. He returned the red frames to his face and then said he'd take my ultimatum to his bosses.

It was the end of the day, so all I could do was log out wondering whether my engineer and I would have a job tomorrow.

Luckily, I didn't have to wait long. The next day, in another Zoom call, my boss told me the engineer would get a 90-day performance improvement plan. I felt a lightness over me. The shaking anxiety was replaced by a steady calm. I smiled to myself. I went to battle for my team member and won. Perhaps the company, upper management, and my boss did value their people.

The 90 days went well. We informed the engineer and he was very receptive. He recognized his weaknesses and was grateful for the opportunity to improve and continue his employment. The three of us together set quantifiable, attainable goals that included improving his coding skills. We met regularly and saw steady improvement. There was one odd thing however: my boss refused to allow him to work on any tasks that had a significant coding component. And yet, during the last month of the improvement plan, both my boss and I had only good feedback for the engineer. So it threw me for an absolute loop that, at the end of the 90 days, my boss still wanted to fire him. His rationale? The coding hadn't improved.

I challenged him: how could he be expected to show coding improvement if we didn't give him any coding to do? Let's say we worked at a toy factory and he had difficulty making teddy bears. How could he improve making bears if he was never given any bears to make? How could we then fire him for not being better at making bears? It was completely illogical.

Then the other shoe dropped: "This engineer was always going to be fired at the end of this 90 days."

Confused, I waited for clarity. He elaborated, "I only allowed the performance improvement plan so that I wouldn't look bad to my boss if you quit."

I sat there stunned, going over the words he said again and again in my head. I slowly started to realize my boss never cared about the engineer, or me, or even the company—only his own position, only himself. Nothing I did mattered. Nothing the engineer did mattered.

This wasn't fair. This was the total opposite of fair. An employee's position, his livelihood, was being thrown away for reasons that had nothing to do with him. How could my boss be so selfish?

Once again I was angry. But more than anger, I felt guilt. Should I have secretly ignored my other responsibilities in order to micromanage this engineer? Should I have hidden the task from upper management? Should I have been dishonest in my critiques, never documenting the areas that he could improve? I've always tried to practice open and honest communication knowing it helps businesses thrive. It helps us collaborate, spot and fix mistakes faster, and improve our skills. But this mistreatment was fostering the opposite. Encouraging me to be closed off and secretive. This was not the right way to treat individuals. This was not the right way to do business.

I formally objected to other authorities within the company, a last-ditch effort to protect the man under my charge, but that only put a target on my back as well. The next day, my boss called me up in that little Zoom window again. It had been determined that I was causing too much trouble and that this engineer's shield needed to be broken as well.

I can't say that I remember the exact words my boss used to fire me. But as I felt the anger well up within me again, I do remember a question swirling around in the back of my head: were my boss and I ever really friends? I had thought we were, but how could he treat me this way if we were friends?

As I wondered this, I suddenly noticed his voice. I really *heard* his voice. Not the words, but the way they were being said. A catch in the throat. A break in the middle of words. Then, I watched as he again removed those red glasses and rubbed his eyes. Was he… crying?

And that's when I started thinking about our chats. I remembered how he told me he just bought a new house and was worried about mortgage payments. I remembered the joy on his face when he said his wife was pregnant and the anxiety he felt about the new baby he had to support. I remembered his worries about his own skills as an engineer and his fear that he'd never be able to land another job if he had to. I thought about the frustration he showed telling me about how unrelenting and arrogant his own boss was and the pressure he felt he was under.

Looking at his face in the call, I felt the shakes of anger dissipate. With a sudden calmness, I cleared my throat. And then I told him it was OK. Told him I understood. Told him that I'd be fine. Told him I enjoyed working with him.

I wanted to console him. Even though I was the one being fired, I wanted him to feel better. Because maybe we were friends. Maybe with the state of corporate culture the way that it is, we are all just doing the best we can. Maybe we're just choosing between the lesser of many evils when we are surrounded by toxic business practices, when profit is all that matters, and when the money our jobs supply is so crucial to our own lives and families.

He smiled from behind those red glasses, thanked me, and ended the call.

To this day, I don't know if we were friends or just coworkers. But I look forward to the day when this is no longer unknown. I look forward to when treating workers with fairness and respect is the norm, and when we don't have to choose between our morals and our job security. I look forward to when we move away from these profit-first, people-last unconscious norms and can feel safe and empowered to do the right things in our workplaces.

Because I believe we are on that path. I believe we can make choices that are right, not just for the business or our pockets, but for each other. I believe that if we continue down this path, our coworkers' actions won't be tainted by fear, but marked by compassion. Perhaps then, friendship can be a certainty.

Until then, I will not let this deter me from fighting for fairness and compassion in my little sphere. But I now will strive to see my coworkers' motivations and not just their actions taken against me. Not to give them an excuse, but to build a bridge through compassionate understanding, and to try to be friends as best as we are able.

The Broken Shield

Kevin Franzman

∽

Kevin Franzman has over ten years of experience in tech and a Master's degree in Computer Science. He has successfully developed apps for multiple industries but his passion is using his experience to help others. Whether volunteering as Director of Technology and Community Operations with Changing Work, or leading software engineering teams to deliver high-quality results in a compassionate and collaborative environment, Kevin believes in making the working world better for workers.

Finding Purpose in Processes

We have entered a new age of fulfillment, in which the great dream is to trade up from money to meaning.

Roman Krznaric

SIXTEEN

Four Questions to Turn Coworkers into Collaborators

Anna Oakes

He cleared his throat loudly. That's when I heard the Southern drawl.

"Uh, hey there everybody. Welcome. And thanks for coming," he boomed. "We're here to learn more about ourselves. And each other. Anna—take it away."

The CEO's introduction may have been short and sweet but I didn't mind. I knew this leadership team had for almost four months been hard at work creating a new vision for the future, exciting their employees, and leveraging their most precious commodity: their employees. "No more bullshit," the CEO challenged his team.

Over the next hour I guided the group in learning about their own strengths and areas of opportunity (which you might call "weaknesses").

"It all starts with self-awareness. Spotting your own strengths helps you get better at spotting strengths in others. And that leads us into our next section—collaboration."

I saw a quick eye-roll as a young woman flipped through her workbook. I get it though. Most trainings suck. Why should mine be any different?

"They'll be no trust falls. We won't practice giving hard

feedback," I said. "But I will teach you four questions that will help you conserve energy, target your strengths strategically, and maximize your impact."

"These four questions have proven themselves over the years that I'd been using them and recommending them to executives and leadership teams. They're simple. They're focused. And incredibly effective."

Preparing for collaboration: Why asking even matters

I've not always been the most deliberate person. I'd spent most of my life operating by gut. I was over 30 when I finally became part of a high-performing team (I'd been on plenty that were just okay) and realized that "I just know" wasn't a legitimate business reason for anyone to invest time or money into my ideas. Deliberative was a strength I hadn't conquered. Yet.

I learned—mostly through failing brilliantly—that being deliberate is crucial for accomplishing whatever you set out to do. It helps you set realistic goals, create roadmaps on how to get there, anticipate challenges you might encounter, and use resources efficiently (things like money, others' time, or your good ideas). Research shows that stopping to consider what you're trying to accomplish helps you integrate new information more quickly and leads to better outcomes.[1] With the volatility of today's world, making informed decisions is essential. And given that most work we do is collaborative, deliberately defining what you're trying to accomplish prevents misunderstandings and ensures teams are all on the same page.

"Use data whenever you can," I told the team. "Deliberate planning relies heavily on empirical data—which is just a fancy way of saying information you gathered from observation or experimentation."

Become a collector of information; of numbers; of trends. What's going on in the world? Your industry? Your company? Your team? Use that, I told them, as the first question: *What are we trying to accomplish?*

Scope your stakeholders: Who will care anyway?

"Maybe you've called them stakeholders before, but why don't we refer to them as 'interested parties'?" I continued. "Because these are the people who will be impacted by what you're trying to accomplish. We don't need fancy titles to consider who will be impacted by the outcome of a project or task. Ask question number two: *Who will care if this happens?*"

Knowing who you're serving can help you gain support for your effort. Consider each person that will need to be informed or consulted—the latter only if they should have a say in the overall direction of the action(s). Alternatively, don't get too carried away and think of everyone as a stakeholder or you won't be able to manage change well. Select the people who are closest to the impact this effort will make.

Consider also where your teams' relationship with this person or group of people is. I use four simple categories when I'm considering the relationship status of who I'm serving:

- **No relationship:** Is it new? Has it failed?
- **Nurturing**: Consider this the courting phase when you're unsure of what direction it will take
- **Developing**: When you know where your relationship is headed and you're on track to get it there
- **Sustaining**: Your relationship is in a great place and there are no barriers to prevent success

Consider those that will be impacted and where your relationship is with them now.

Define which of these four phases it's in now, then where you want it to be. Be wise though, not every relationship will be sustaining and some may backtrack at times. The boss who you would have categorized as "sustaining" could suddenly shift to "nurturing" after they're assigned two new teams. The goal here is to simply pay attention to where they are, where you need them to be for this change to happen, and what you can do to get them there.

Manage perception: What will they say about you when you aren't around?

I live in the United States, in the Midwest near Lake Michigan. People in these parts are what we call "Midwest nice". We're raised not to brag, to put others before ourselves, and to be humble. And there's a case for that. Research shows that humble leaders do inspire others to step up.[2] But being humble doesn't mean you shouldn't consider your impact on others. There's a difference between self-awareness and bragging. And this series of questions, specifically the third question, sets you up to consider what they'll say about you when you aren't around: *How do I want to be perceived?*

"If you're struggling with this question, consider what you want people to say about you after this effort is accomplished," I guided. "What natural strengths do you want on full display? And when you're working with others, consider how each of you would like to be perceived."

A quiet man in his late fifties spoke up. "Well I don't like to brag now," he crooned. See? Midwest nice.

I knew there were likely others still struggling with this question so I opened it up further. "Let's flip our thinking. Intent and perception go hand in hand," I said. "How you want them to feel will direct how you show up, and therefore how you will be perceived. Your natural strengths will shine."

"What if I don't know how to articulate my natural strengths?" interrupted a dark-haired woman from across the room. I assured her that this indeed is why we're here. To learn about what we're great at and how to operate from those zones as often as possible.

Syncing up: Pairing your strengths with others

The fourth and final question: *What strengths should we lead with?* Given the answers to the first three—what you are trying to accomplish, who will be impacted by the efforts, and how you'd each like to be perceived—what natural talents will you choose to lead with? How will they complement each other? How are they stronger when pairing them together?

I paused to allow the group to absorb the significance of this final question. "This is where the magic happens," I said, my eyes scanning the room. "This is where we take everything we've learned about ourselves and our goals, and we create a symphony of strengths."

Research[3] has consistently shown that teams who focus on leveraging individual strengths outperform those who don't. A Gallup study[4] found that people who use their strengths every day are six times more likely to be engaged in their jobs. But it's not just about individual performance—it's about how these strengths work together.

"Think of it like a jigsaw puzzle," I continued. "Each piece has its unique shape and color but it's only when we fit them together that we see the full picture. That's what we're doing with our strengths."

I walked over to the whiteboard and started writing. "Let's take an example. Say we're trying to launch a new product. We've identified our key stakeholders as the marketing team, the sales department, and our top clients. We want to be perceived as innovative, reliable, and customer-focused."

I turned back to the group. "Now, what strengths should we lead with? Maybe we need someone with strong strategic thinking to plan. We might want someone with a propensity for action to get things moving quickly. Perhaps we need someone with high empathy to understand and address customer concerns."

The room was buzzing now, people nodding and whispering to each other. I could see the lightbulbs going off.

"But here's the key," I said, raising my voice slightly to regain their attention. "It's not just about identifying these strengths. It's about understanding how they work together. How does the strategic thinker's long-term vision complement the let's-get-started desire for immediate action? How can the empathetic team member help both of them understand the customer's perspective?"

I let that sink in for a moment before continuing. "This is where true collaboration happens. It's not about everyone doing everything. It's about each person bringing their unique strengths to the table and finding ways to amplify each other's talents."

Research[5] from the *Harvard Business Review* supports this approach. They found that diverse teams are smarter and more innovative—but only when they're managed in a way that values each member's unique contribution.

"So as you consider this fourth question," I concluded, "think beyond just listing strengths. Think about how these strengths interact. How can they balance each other out? How can they create something greater than the sum of their parts?"

The room was silent for a moment then erupted into discussion. I smiled, knowing that they were beginning to see the power of this approach. They were starting to understand that true collaboration isn't about everyone doing the same thing—it's about everyone bringing their best selves to the table and working together in harmony.

As the chatter continued I knew this team was on the path to something great. They were learning to see not just their own strengths, but the strengths of others. And in doing so they were unlocking the true potential of their team.

Making this work for you

Throughout my career I've witnessed countless teams struggle with collaboration not because they lacked talent, but because they never took the time to understand how their individual strengths could complement one another. These four questions—what are we trying to accomplish, who will care, how do we want to be perceived, and what strengths should we lead with—have transformed not just my approach to teamwork but my entire professional outlook. What began as a solution to my own frustration with "just okay" teams became a framework that has helped leaders across industries build truly exceptional collaborative environments.

I invite you to experiment with these questions in your next meeting or project kickoff. Start small if you need to—perhaps just by clarifying what you're trying to accomplish and identifying one strength you want to lead with. You might be surprised at how quickly these simple inquiries can shift team dynamics from competitive to collaborative and from draining to energizing. Remember, effective collaboration isn't about forcing everyone to contribute equally to every task; it's about creating a space where each person's unique talents can shine and interlock with others to create something truly remarkable.

The most powerful teams don't just work together—they amplify each other's brilliance.

Anna Oakes

∽

Anna Oakes has dedicated her career to improving the world of work. From helping companies build strong company culture, operationalizing culture, and nurturing intrapreneurs, Anna acts as a growth sherpa for small and mid-sized companies that want to drive both productivity and flourishing.

SEVENTEEN

Deep and Dynamic: Designing Beyond a 2D Workplace

Mary McDowall

It's a Friday in early March. The late morning sun is filling my dining room and giving the illusion of warmth on this wintery day. I'm at home, alone, as I have the day off work. I'm thinking of calling a friend to suggest we go out for lunch.

Then in an instant everything changes.

To begin, the change is almost imperceptible, like that first nudge of an intuitive whisper. Then it's as if someone is turning out the lights in a naturally lit room. Suddenly the shift is palpable, as if I'm being wrapped in a shroud of dense dread. It rises, silently, like the early morning mist off a still lake. It feels heavy, bordering on suffocating. Panic kicks in. My heart rate escalates and I begin to feel detached from my body. I'm scared. Something is not right, but I don't know what.

Nothing in my physical surroundings has changed but I have the sensation of a rug being pulled out from beneath me. Instead of the hardwood floor there is a gaping black chasm below my feet. My body tries to rebalance, to recalibrate, pedaling madly—like Wile E. Coyote just before he plunges over a cliff. My feet are seeking solid ground but I'm actually standing perfectly still. My mind is blank.

Then I hear a voice. It's in my head. A calm and authoritative voice.

"Get help. Now!"

With effort, I look and try to focus on the phone attached to the wall. It's only about five steps away, but appears unreachable. Time blurs and I'm reaching for the phone, my fingers automatically pushing the buttons for the number of my local doctor's office. Over a decade later, I do not know why I didn't call my friend, or my mother, or my husband.

The voice that speaks into the receiver is faint, distant, and barely recognizable as my own.

"I can't go back to work."

It's an illogical thing to say, as I don't need to be at work until Monday. But the receptionist who answers my call must have heard something in the tone of my voice, because within the hour I was sitting in my doctor's office. He suggests I take a couple of weeks off work. I voice my concern. I'm involved in a specially funded project and we're planning a community event that's due to take place in three weeks. People are counting on me.

He suggests I lengthen my leave of absence until after the event is over. I honestly don't know if I'm more distressed by what just happened or by the thought of letting down my employer and co-workers.

The year is 2012. I'm working part-time as a volunteer coordinator for a community mental health agency that serves a rural area about the size of Scotland. I enjoy my job and the many perks that come with it. I am privileged to work with staff across four regional offices, from managers and volunteers to clerical and front-line staff. My manager works in a different town so I have a sizable degree of autonomy and a flexible work week. I can set my own hours. My workdays are full and my responsibilities varied. I feel I am contributing to the agency's purpose and being of service to my coworkers. I was completely caught off guard when my mental health took a nosedive.

Those three weeks of medical leave turn into nine months.

Burnout is a bitch. Recovery takes more time than I expect. Eventually I begin to think about returning to my place of employment. On paper the decision is easy. I like my job, my co-workers, it fits my skill set, and my desire to be of service. Yet something is holding me back. That feeling of dread seeps in when I visualize myself back at my desk. I decide to listen to this instinctual knowing and after a few tearful calls I tell my manager that I won't be coming back to work.

The unanticipated result of my decision was that along with my job my connection to all but a few close co-workers was severed. My manager sent a personalized announcement of my employment termination to the agency staff. As I would learn later, after a chance encounter with an out-of-town manager, due to agency privacy policies no one, not even the program managers, knew any details. To them I simply disappeared into that abyss that claims so many not-for-profit employees.

The year is 2025, and I have been working online for twelve years as a solopreneur, or a co-creativepreneur, as I prefer to call myself. My current co-workers are my two border collie companions, Kap and Remy. Some people may think working from home is lonely or isolating. I've found just the opposite. Working virtually, I can connect and cocreate with a host of people who I wouldn't have met otherwise.

Having lost the structure of an external office and the somewhat artificial construct of a social network of co-workers, I am free to create and nurture my own work relationships. Along with improvements in technology that eliminate the restrictions of location and travel, I'm able to consciously choose who I collaborate with, who I coach, and who I turn to for support and advice. My virtual work relationships are deep and dynamic and go beyond the perceived limitations of connecting via a two-dimensional screen.

Five design elements for deep and dynamic 2D connections

Intention. One of the first people I formed an intentional and close working relationship with was Jewelz. We met in 2013 through a coaching training, when we were paired as practice coaching partners. Jewelz comes from a corporate background. She's ten years older than me, lives in a different country, and is two times zones away. We set an intention to continue supporting each other as coaches but our relationship transcends work and technology. For twelve years we have been meeting more weeks than not. She is wise and wonderful and my Wednesdays don't feel right without our connection. I know her as a true and valued friend, a confidante, coach, client, sounding board, source of creative inspiration, and so much more. We have never met in person.

Imagination. I met Kathy through my coaching affiliation. As master coaches Kathy and I had the opportunity to create a complementary program. Initially we developed a facilitator training to lead a kinder approach to masterminding. We enjoyed working together and soon expanded our collaboration. Some weeks we met almost daily, each from our respective homes and countries.

One day, feeling a little stuck, we took a screen break. When we returned The Purple Ink Café was born. At first it was just an imaginative construct that created a tangible, albeit virtual, place for us to meet. It soon took on a life of its own. When we held workshops and trainings we invited the participants to join us at The Purple Ink Café. Using a guided relaxation, we invited them to create their own version of what this space looked and felt like.

As the years progressed Kathy and I have become more than colleagues and collaborators: we're good friends with many shared interests. And when the time came that our interests diverged, we made the decision to let go of our delightful café. It was difficult, but our friendship and mutual respect made the transition easier. Our connection though did not end.

We continue to this day to host a co-working session most Monday mornings in a new imaginative space called The Room of Perpetual Inspiration. The women who regularly join us have formed a welcoming community with friendships and connections of their own. In addition to Monday mornings, we still meet with our master mind facilitators once a month in the VIP Lounge, a speak-easy type room within The Purple Ink Cafe. Guided relaxations bring us into a place of presence and connection and bring an added imaginative energy to our masterminds.

Ingenuity. Because I'm an introvert it can be easy for me to fade towards invisible while on a large or impersonal Zoom call. Cultivating a personal connection on screens filled with boxes of unfamiliar faces can be hard. Combining intention with a bit of ingenuity has led to some genuine and beneficial connections. When attending an online course or workshop, especially one with lots of participants, I've learned to stay open and curious about my intuitive and energetic attraction to individuals on the call. I make a note of their name before returning my focus to the content of the call.

I am both delighted and intrigued by how often this simple technique has turned into opportunities for working with someone who would not normally have crossed my path. Some connections were instant while others happened years later. Like traditional working relationships some were time limited, and others continue into the unforeseeable future.

Integrity. Sara Marie is a fiery and sassy double Aries who exudes both passion and compassion. We 'met' during a year-long online priestess program. I was naturally drawn to her energy, which feels like a breath of fresh air. She is also real, with real life issues and challenges, and an openness and curiosity for life that prompted me to make a note of her name. After the program was over our connection was lost. Or so I thought.

Three years later, in 2024, a mutual friend unintentionally reconnected us when she invited Sara Marie to join our Monday morning co-working community. Sara Marie continued to attend despite it being at 6:30 a.m. her time. In March I held a call to talk about inner peace. She was the only one to attend. Our conversation was dynamic and engaging. It felt so natural, as if we weren't talking into a monitor to someone in a different country and three time zones away, but sitting at a kitchen table enjoying a cup of tea.

The integrity of that conversation, of her spirit, and our shared interests in the full scope of the Yogic philosophy for living, had a resonating effect. Intuitively I knew there was real potential for a partnership of some kind.

Intuition. Taking a risk in business isn't just financial nor is it all based on facts. Intuition plays an important role in conscious collaborations. Sara Marie and I continued to meet and in the summer we began offering a monthly event for people to come together and talk about real issues through the lens of inner peace. Another imaginative space materialized, called The Sacred Oasis. It likely didn't make sense on paper but intuitively we each knew our vision had real potential. By the end of 2024 our synchronistic reconnection had grown into an online, heart-led community, which creates a safe, sacred, and welcoming space for people to show up just as they are and feel included and valued.

Designing depth in two dimensions

I jokingly refer to my virtual colleagues as my 2D friends, though the depth of our connection is fully embodied. Distance and dimension do not need to limit or define your relationships. If you work alone, whether by choice or circumstance, your working relationships have an equal if not greater possibility to be as deep, meaningful, and rewarding as those with co-workers you see in person. Advances in technology allow for a multitude of connections that bridge time zones and eliminate the barrier of distance. Develop your connections with intention, imagination, ingenuity, integrity, and intuition to create your own online, international, multicultural extravaganza!

That dark chasm that shadowed me in 2012 is now as dim as the faint light I first followed back to health. Today I'm able to let my inner light shine. Burnout, or any health issue, are not easy, but my experience expanded my work and world to include the wonderful, varied, interesting, capable, and engaging people whom I am happy to call my friends and co-creative colleagues.

The words of Donna, my client, collaborator, colleague, and friend sum it up beautifully. "The bottom line, it's kind of hard for me to remember that we have never met in person, because you are such a good friend!"

Mary McDowall

∾

Mary McDowall is a co-creativepreneur, a multi-certified coach, a small group facilitator and course creator. She weaves the essence of kaizen, the play of creativity, and the spirit of Vedic wisdom into all her offerings. Mary is the co-founder of The Sacred Oasis: a gathering place for heart-led humans, and a graduate of and community leader for the Inner MBA program. She lives in her hometown of Parry Sound, Ontario.

EIGHTEEN

GIRLIE, This Isn't a Family Affair!

Erem Latif

Like most people, I have experienced multiple versions of professional relationships. True and lasting connections which turned into friendship. Power jockeying that created uncomfortable workplace politics. And the ultimate icing on the cake: toxic gossip-mongering which shifted into unethical management by a trusted mentor.

Across all these relationships I've felt the normal range of emotions: from elation and connection to confusion, anxiety, mistrust, and finally outright violation and bewilderment.

Most workplace relationships fall within these categories. While the Niagara Institute categorizes work relationships according to four simplistic categories—reporting organizational, friendship, or personal—I feel these are mere guidelines and work relationships have become infinitely more nuanced.[1] Furthermore, they are contingent on the emotional maturity and intelligence of all those involved.

While workplace relationship principles may be a topic covered in many graduate schools and business or social science classes, I don't believe many retain this information after spending years in the workforce. And many simply don't truly grasp the application of these principles in the real world.

To that end, I'd like to share an approach that I've cultivated over the years. It's simple, effective, and based solely on the following guiding principles: goal, intention, role, and ethics—or GIRLIE. These categories serve to build work relationships, behaviors, and daily conversations on foundations of trust, support, and reliance, while ensuring we are aligned with our truest and most authentic selves.

Before diving into the GIRLIE concept, I'll start with the latter statement and ethos first: alignment and authenticity. While these words mean different things to different groups of people, I think we've all experienced moments where we *knew* in our heart of hearts that whatever activity, discussion, or thought process we were engaged in at the time, was a true reflection of our truest, most authentic selves. Those moments of true alignment are what I request that you begin with in order to build truly meaningful relationships, especially in the workplace, where boundaries get clouded, competition is palpable, and not everyone is bringing forward their most authentic or truest self. I find that if we begin with personal alignment and that associated level of integrity, addressing each of the relationship concepts become natural and intuitive, which then guides true connection from role to role and company to company.

Now let's dive into GIRLIE.

The G represents the word Goal. When we set an intention of forming a connection with a coworker, we inevitably develop a goal or purpose for doing so. For example, if I intend to connect with my team members because we are all working toward a common goal or product, the underlying goal is focused on ideation, collaboration, and efficient and effective delivery. The beautiful thing that may happen as a byproduct of this goal is the forging of a friendship that outlasts the given project or tenures at a given company. If you work at a larger organization with a wider umbrella of benefits, such as book clubs, walking groups, or carpools—you connect with those individuals based on a shared interest (or need, in the case of the carpool). These specific group dynamics then create the goals for those groups.

A consideration that dovetails nicely with Goal is Intention, the I in GIRLIE. Goal and Intention are two different sides of the same coin. We humans, consciously or unconsciously, set intentions for any given relationship. From my own perspective, and based on input from those around me, this step can be overlooked and is frequently ignored—but it is desperately needed. There is a power behind an intention. It provides direction, a guide, if you will for the nature of the relationship moving forward.

To better understand this, take any example from your personal life, whether it be your mother or your father, your brother or sister, or your spouse or significant other. There is a known social factor of what's needed, what's required, and what's expected for each of these relational paradigms. But because similar definitions don't exist in the workplace, we are left shrugging our shoulders and looking blankly at our colleagues. By setting an intention one's behavior, words, and actions can be guided.

Back to the example shared earlier, when considering my team goals I will work not only toward my individual success but also foster group success on a project. My intention for success is driving my engagement with my team members—which can look as simple as coming into work and helping motivate or inspire team members during a team discussion. "I had a great idea this weekend while I was working in the garden. What if we applied concept X to problem Y?" Conversely, in the book club example, the intention is to connect or engage with coworkers who share the same interest or love in reading. That intention helps by guiding how we are relating to our colleagues in an environment separate from a team—there is a mental collaboration, or an intellectual connection, that forms the basis for behaviors, words, and actions in these types of connections. The fact that the members of the book club are technically coworkers becomes irrelevant.

The R in GIRLIE is for Role. As you consider any workplace relationship, it is logical to consider your role and the role of your colleague. Various levels of positions, reporting structures, and team goals can impact the quality of the connection and the dynamic of the relationship. A managerial role, in which one person serves as the manager to whom the other reports, automatically creates certain boundaries. While this dynamic has some standard guidelines on behaviors of engagement, we do get the opportunity to leverage the first two principles, Goal and Intention, in how we act as managers.

A more consciously directed manager can set an intention to act as a true mentor, supporter, and guide, using their experience as an asset to the direct report. In this case the goal would be to help the employee grow, flourish, and succeed. The manager would be clearly using their position for the benefit of the relationship and the team. On the opposite end of the spectrum, collegial roles create a more open environment—one based on building true connection, trust, and reliance with another human. Friendships can be fostered that may very well spill over into personal lives. I've had the great fortune to experience a few of these in my own career. While the original thread of the relationship was coworker-based, our relationships blossomed into lasting bonds of friendships based on connection, growth, and support.

The final point to consider is E, for Ethics. Ethics is a standard that directs the conduct of individuals and society. As we forge relationships in a work environment, goals and intentions are driven by one's ethical standards. Returning to our earlier examples, my goal and intention to develop a connection with team members to improve and support optimum performance is driven by my ethics of wanting to put forth my own best professional effort. In parallel, I recognize that my team members and I are already colleagues and coworkers, a thread that already unites us. But weaving a stronger connection into a tapestry that highlights the strength of the team, benefits all who are directly involved as well as leadership (who indirectly might be awaiting the completion of the project). By evaluating the ethics behind my goals and intentions, I am also leveraging my own emotional maturity and emotional intelligence—both qualities that can be overlooked in the workplace and which can't be captured by a résumé.

Emotional intelligence is the ability to manage AND understand your emotions, while also recognizing and influencing the emotions of others around you.[2] An individual with high emotional intelligence would be empathic, an effective communicator, self-aware, motivated, and have the ability to self-regulate as situations call for it.

There are behaviors one can cultivate in order to improve emotional intelligence, the first of which is to learn emotional vocabulary. This translates to things like using words such as "frustrated", "overwhelmed", or "indifferent"—instead of "bad" in the phrase 'I feel bad'.

One can also learn to engage better with others by strengthening one's social skills. How do I achieve this you ask? Practice. On a weekly basis, set time aside to practice holding eye contact, nodding to evoke engagement, and offering open-ended questions. We all hate it sometimes, but small talk does offer the opportunity of connection. Asking about family, recreational time and activities, and even occupation, provides a means of interest and therefore connection. Another component of building emotional intelligence is the body scan. By evaluating certain body parts—breath, jaw, and breath again—for five or ten seconds, one can gauge one's own mental state and mitigate tension that might impact communication or interaction. Finally, just as self-awareness allows one to feel tense areas of the body, becoming more aware of micro-expressions in others provides infinite information on their emotions. Eyebrow raises, pursed or tight lips, crossed arms, or leaning in—share volumes about how others may be feeling during a conversation or meeting.

Taking that one step further, emotional maturity is loosely defined as the ability to not only manage but understand our own emotions effectively, thereby allowing us to build and sustain healthy relationships. Emotional maturity is an active effort, a constant work in progress, where one is not only becoming aware of one's emotions but is also coping with random situations based on the understanding of those emotions. Behaviors associated with emotional maturity include flexibility, taking ownership and/or responsibility as needed, seeking growth or expansion from any situation, resiliency, maintaining a calm disposition, and being approachable.[3]

The fundamental difference between the two centers on understanding versus acting—the intelligence aspect versus the engagement effort. Many leaders may be evaluated for emotional intelligence before taking a high-profile leadership role, but may lack emotional maturity. The latter allows us to navigate complex social situations and forms the foundation of being able to identify goal, role, and intention—and ultimately to act ethically in every workplace relationship.

Tying this all together, relationships in the workplace can be built on various foundations with multiple goals as their driving force. As emotionally intelligent and emotionally mature individuals, we need certain skill sets to be able to identify our own feelings, emotions, and motivations. Because these relationships are distinctively different to the personal relationships in which we may have more latitude on what we tolerate versus what we resist—navigation can be challenging, tricky, and sometimes unbearable. The keys to managing these relationships are established by a conscious decision on one's part to truly behave with intention, based on relationship goals, team roles, and one's underlying ethical standards.

Erem Latif

~

Erem Latif is a best-selling author, writer, speaker, and consultant with twenty years' success in driving human performance and whole health optimization using neuroscience marketing, behavioral health methodologies, and engagement-driven solutions. Erem continues to champion compassionate leadership, employee wellness, and soul-driven connection in her professional efforts. She has an MS in Biomedical Science and an MBA in Healthcare Management.

NINETEEN

From Friction to Flow: Using Your Human Operating System

Lori Kirkland

The tension in the room was suffocating.

Sitting in a full-day workshop with fifteen other Financial Tech professionals, it felt like the air had thickened and was pressing against my chest. Within an hour of kickoff, the energy of the room had turned heavy. Tommy, a smart strategist, was turning what was supposed to be a collaborative workshop into his own personal playback of his roadmap.

My mind was racing. *Is this why I have worked so hard my whole career? To have someone with limited view of the whole picture be demanding, so we only do what he wants?* After reminding him three times that there was work well beyond his entrance to the project I was tired of being batted back. Tommy doubled down by saying his start date… again. I could feel my energy matching his and him throwing back even more defensive tones. I began to freeze up as eight people, on the earlier projects, started to display tense muscles and their body energy signaled distress. At the same time it felt like their eyes began to focus on me to see what I was going to do.

I was a senior leader in the meeting, one of two team members of the executive team present. My mind began to scramble with panic as I realized that even though the other leader was Tommy's boss, his way of working was to stay quiet until he knew exactly what to do. I was the people person, the one who was fluid with moving people toward a common goal. I could see that others were waiting for my action as the room fatigued with the high-pressure push from Tommy.

Robbie spoke up, frustration evident in her voice as she described how she felt that Tommy would bully his way through the workshop until he got exactly what he wanted. Across the room I noticed how Grant shifted uncomfortably in his seat, tugging at his shirt, organizing, and reorganizing the items in front of him. Nadia attempted to interject with direct points and thoughts on the topic, but her voice lacked the force to match Tommy's dominance. Sparrow asked, "Can you clarify this subject and how it aligns with the way the customers want to give?" She was trying to bring in the group and gain alignment within it but was given a brush off response. Internally I was boiling! I felt a sense of unfairness and of rudeness. Most of all I felt the uncomfortable energy that was radiating from everyone in the room.

Then it dawned on me: so many people become disengaged at work because the effort to change the energy is so hard to overcome. The biggest takeaway? **Energy matters.**

Tommy could sense our desire to contribute but he pushed on anyway, his body twitching slightly as he spoke with an even stronger tone, determined to make sure his perspectives were heard above all others. As I took it all in, my heart pounded loudly and my throat tightened. A wave of sadness hit me: this was supposed to be a collaborative effort but it had turned into a one-man show driven by ego rather than a shared group goal. The energy in the room was filled with frustration and unspoken tension.

Seeing these patterns play out in real time highlighted for me that we all have automatic responses when we encounter discomfort in the workplace. These responses—shaped by our personal histories and professional experiences in our Human Operating System (HuOS)—become patterns and influence the energy we bring into a room. The struggle in the meeting wasn't because people didn't know better. It was because one person's dominance took precedence over the group working toward a bigger goal.

And while Tommy is crazy smart, his short-sightedness of the people aspect of business made it clear to me that relationships at work are way beyond processes, planning, and expertise. For over a century, business has operated with metrics that are logical and analytical, but those miss the energy of the people.

In that moment it was clear: this room needed a disruption. *Do I apply the same pressure? Reciprocate the aggression?* As a woman in tech, I have had competitive showdowns more than I care to admit. But truthfully, I didn't want to play the silly power game those required.

As I've gotten older I've realized that while I can assert dominance and push back, it never feels right. I'm not one of those people who avoids confrontation. In fact I rarely shy away—even though there are many examples where I probably should have. My past patterns helped me recognize that with the uneasy tension in the room, pursuing confrontation that wasn't in alignment with what I value wouldn't get me to where I wanted. I thrive on optimism and always search for a win-win, not just a win.

But I was getting anxious. Tommy's ego was locked in a battle to be right, clinging to his list and processes while shutting out everyone else. As the room tried to shift the energy, he only grew louder, more aggressive, and more dominant—almost as if our attempts to interject were fueling his need to take control—even though all we wanted was a little lightness.

Instinctively I approached the situation the way I always do when faced with a complex challenge—like debugging a software program. If I could understand the energy patterns beneath the surface, maybe I could shift the energy and get us all unstuck. First I had to regulate my own Human Operating System (HuOS). I noticed my body on high alert—tight muscles, rapid heartbeat—so I paused to reset. Using deep breathing, I calmed my nervous system, shifting from fight-or-flight to a state of clarity and intention and getting myself grounded.

Once centered, I stepped back to observe the room. Each person was reacting from their own ingrained patterns. Dan, the leader, was taking notes, appearing disengaged but likely deep in thought. Adnon, the facilitator, worked around the room looking to find a way to relieve the stress. Meanwhile instant messages reflected the growing tension. One was particularly clear: "This is bad. We need to stop this."

At that moment I saw two choices—step back and let the chaos continue or intervene and try to shift the energy. I chose the latter. Instead of confronting Tommy with resistance I interrupted with curiosity. "What's the most important thing you want us all to take away from this?" I asked, making space for him to be heard while redirecting the conversation. Once he answered, I called a break, giving everyone a moment to reset.

All that tension brought back memories of a similar project in terms of complexity and setup, but with a completely different experience. Working on an airline project, I remembered how challenging it was. It pushed my intellect beyond what I thought possible, demanding countless hours of intense problem-solving. And despite the difficulty, the team fostered an atmosphere of ease, strength, and mutual support.

We upheld high standards, meeting deadlines and delivering results with integrity—but the real magic was in our shared commitment to solving problems for the greater good. Collaboration, experimentation, and creativity thrived alongside rigorous logical analysis because we trusted that everyone was operating with the best intentions.

Yes, we worked long hours—probably too long—but the team itself became a source of energy and growth. It wasn't just about getting the job done; it was about being part of something bigger than any one of us. And that felt *awesome!*

The difference between resistance and flow in teams

I started reflecting on the dichotomy of the two experiences. How could two situations, so similar in structure and demands, create such drastically different environments?

One felt stifled, as if there wasn't enough space in the conversation for everyone. Frustration and disengagement settled in, defenses went up, and the meeting became more about getting through it than about achieving real outcomes. Even though everyone spoke in professional tones the energy in the room told a different story—it was tense, forced, and anything but natural.

In contrast, the other group moved like a well-rehearsed crew. While we weren't necessarily friends, there was mutual respect. We shared a common goal, working together to improve our small corner of the world. There was no posturing, no hidden agendas—just a team aligned in its purpose. Conversations were productive and people engaged freely, knowing they could contribute without fear of judgment or retaliation. The tone was friendly, the dialogue open, and ideas flowed effortlessly.

Realizing that the energy at play was helping define a workplace situation made me see: it isn't just about words, processes, or even personalities. Rather it's the way the ideas are communicated, the energy that supports the ideas, and the ability to move toward a goal bigger than any one person. Energy moves in patterns between people. You're always giving off energy and receiving it from those around you. Group dynamics of teams contain the culmination of the individual energies coming together to form a bigger atmosphere. Understanding this gives you power within any circumstance. If you can change your own energy, you can shift the energy of the group at any time.

In the first team, words were professional but the energy was fractured. Communication felt disjointed, which fueled tension, defensiveness, and exhaustion. People operated in survival mode and were stuck in rigid patterns that made collaboration feel forced. It became clear that this wasn't just one bad meeting—it was the team's default mode of operation. Our energy exchange had been dictated by norms that had long been in place. Overbooked calendars left no room for deep thinking, which led to stress and burnout. The process-over-outcomes mindset meant the plan mattered more than results, which shut down creative or efficient alternatives. A focus on the activity-over-impact mentality led to measuring busyness instead of meaningful progress, and to team members checking boxes rather than focusing on the bigger picture.

The airline team on the other hand, moved with clarity, trust, and alignment because their energy flowed freely. Big-picture-thinking kept the focus on meaningful outcomes rather than rigid adherence to process, and this led to an awareness that multiple solutions were always possible. Conversations about those possibilities led to teamwork and bonding. Resilience and adaptability developed when the energy allowed the team to pivot when challenges arose, using setbacks as opportunities for growth. Rhythmic momentum of a steady cadence kept the team in sync, creating the energetic freedom to explore, learn, and fail.

In life we will always encounter situations that challenge us. By recognizing the energy we bring into a space we gain the power to shape our response to those situations. Our energy influences those around us and by shifting it intentionally, we can transform not only our experience but the entire dynamic of a team.

Shifting workplace dynamics with your HuOS

Each of us has the power to decide where and how we direct our energy. When we let struggles take over our mental space—like replaying a tough meeting in our minds—we're unintentionally giving that experience more energy than it deserves.

At our core, each of us operates a Human Operating System (HuOS)—a unique internal framework of operating patterns shaped by our biology, experiences, and survival instincts. The patterns we run aren't inherently right or wrong—they simply are. By taking inventory of our own energy we can more easily observe the energy of others and find new and often unplanned possibilities.

Workplace relationships function like a neural network—strong, connected teams adapt quickly while unresolved tension creates cognitive interference and slows everything down. But tension itself isn't the problem. In fact it's a signal—friction between perspectives that, when harnessed correctly, leads to sharper decision-making.

Cognitively diverse and flexible teams outperform those that avoid conflict altogether. The goal isn't harmony—it's productive friction. True adaptability happens when individuals and teams learn to hold tension, process it intelligently, and emerge with solutions stronger than any single perspective could have created alone.

When we step back and simply observe, without judgment, we unlock the power to shift, adapt, and create environments where energy flows freely instead of getting stuck. Looking at the two teams, I realized they shared many of the same tasks and challenges, yet the way they approached them made all the difference. Some embraced the **human** element in business, which created flow, while others operated against the energy present, and created friction:

- (H) Having the observer's mindset: Effective teams trust the process and each other. Shifting from control to adaptability helps you recognize energy patterns at play. Instead of reacting with judgment, an observer's mindset fosters curiosity—allowing you to influence dynamics for better outcomes.
- (U) Understanding your value and purpose: Amid constant demands, grounding yourself in your purpose cuts through the noise. When you embody your values, it inspires others—turns exhaustion into excitement and routine into motivation. Purpose-driven energy transforms interactions from transactional to meaningful.
- (M) Micro-moments of choice: Every interaction offers a choice: react on autopilot or respond intentionally. Recognizing patterns in yourself and others gives you the power to disrupt negative cycles. Small shifts compound, reshaping relationships and strengthening team dynamics.
- (A) Awareness as a reset button: The simplest way to break a pattern? Awareness. A single deep breath can restore clarity, shifting energy from tension to resolution

within your HuOS. Your ability to reset in the moment determines the trajectory of conversations and outcomes.

- (N) Noticing patterns and breaking free: Recognizing patterns is like strengthening a muscle—the more you practice, the easier it becomes. When frustration arises ask: *Is this about the present, or something deeper?* Awareness gives you the power to break cycles—not just in meetings but in life.

Tapping into the tools already built into our HuOS isn't just about managing ourselves—it's about reading the unspoken energy in a room and using it to create real change. The need to label a coworker as a friend or just an acquaintance starts to fade because when we show up authentically and allow others to do the same, the boundaries that friendships typically provide for safety naturally become unnecessary. When trust and openness flow freely, connection isn't forced—it just happens.

When teams recognize their patterns—both individually and collectively—they gain the power to turn tension into productive friction, not by avoiding conflict, but by channeling it toward alignment and progress. Sometimes all it takes is one intentional shift to move from stuck to unstuck, and to turn friction into flow.

Lori Kirkland

Lori Kirkland is a conscious leader, transformation expert, and co-founder of DeepHumanX. With over 25 years in tech and business evolution, she helps leaders stay relevant by blending human strengths with AI to drive innovation in creating positive systems of change. Passionate about adaptive leadership, she empowers leaders to navigate change and challenge assumptions. She lives in beautiful Colorado with her two amazing daughters, balancing deep thinking, mountain air, and just the right amount of caffeine.

TWENTY

Transforming Isolation into Connection: A Practitioner's Guide

Wendy McHenry

I sat in the sparse waiting room for an eternity before a job interview. Finally Julie came out to greet me. She was dressed in a black blazer, white button-down shirt, black slacks and black shoes —her hair in a perfect tight bun. She held the door open for me and I got a whiff of the stale air from the office floor.

Its large open space revealed an open cubicle floor plan with no walls—no privacy—everyone sitting inches away from each other.

As Julie's heels click-clacked on the floor she pointed out the coffee break room, where the overbearing fluorescent lights hummed a little too loudly. As I toured the office I got the feeling that her no-nonsense business uniform was not the only thing that was so formal, so corporate, so *sterile*. It felt like a never-ending array of cubicles, like I was in the Apple TV+ show *Severance*.

"Who on earth would willingly work in a place like this?" I thought to myself at the end of the interview.

Turns out *I* would work in a place like that—and I did, for almost five years. I desperately needed that job.

I sat inches away from my co-workers every day from 8:30 to 5:30 and the formality I had previewed when meeting Julie held true for much of my time there. We were there to work, not to socialize, and despite how physically close we were, we didn't know each other except for what was needed to get the job done.

This meant the pain I carried—when my father had his stroke, when I had a miscarriage, when my husband went through a health crisis—I carried alone. Very few people at the office knew what was happening, if any knew at all.

Despite being near my colleagues, I felt very alone and isolated and struggled to make it through each day.

Flash forward to a more recent work experience.

When walking into the expansive and elegant ballroom at the Disney Coronado Springs Resort in Orlando I was hit with a wave of air conditioning even though it was February. A nervous energy was pulsating through the crowd and I could hear exclamations above the hum of the crowd as people greeted each other with excitement. Nervously I glanced around, trying to spot a familiar face. Then I landed on a colleague across the way and made a beeline for her.

I gave Sandra a big hug. We had spent countless hours working together, not only on our regular day-to-day work but on planning this special meeting event. People flew in from all over the world to be there together.

She joked, "It's so great to finally meet you!"

We laughed and giggled as we caught up. I pinched myself—how could she know me so well even though this was the first time I was experiencing her in three dimensions?

After leaving the cubicle-farm job, I had moved into a career where my colleagues and I are spread across the country, sometimes across the globe. The majority of the time I work from home and alone—I was working remotely long before the pandemic made it common.

So how did I feel so lonely when I was in a cubicle environment, physically near my coworkers—yet so connected to my coworkers in a different job even though we were spread across the globe?

The answer lies in how organizations purposefully create opportunities for connection and cultivate an environment that supports building authentic connections at work.

. . .

In my experience, an extremely effective way of building authentic connections at work has been via Employee Resource Groups (ERGs). ERGs have provided a sense of community while providing meaning and purpose in the work. ERGs offer an opportunity to build authentic relationships with co-workers that cross all segments of title, department, salary, and tenure.

According to Kalina Bryant, "ERGs serve as catalysts for community building within organizations. ... These groups provide a welcoming space where employees with shared backgrounds or interests can come together, connect, and share their experiences. This sense of belonging is crucial for employee engagement, job satisfaction, and overall well-being."[1]

A key component of fostering this connection can simply be through networking events, whether in person or virtually, where people have the chance to get to know each other outside of what they contribute at work. A popular format I have used for my global group is to provide a panel discussion on the topic at hand (for example topics pertaining to International Women's Day, Black History Month, or Pride Month) followed by an opportunity for networking. This format works both virtually or in person. I have met incredible friends and mentors through virtual networking sessions over recent years! I wish the same for each of you.

I first became involved in ERGs as a volunteer in 2016. By 2019 I was a co-founder of an ERG supporting women in the workplace and by 2023 I was Chair of a Global ERG for my industry group, supporting women in tech. My ever-increasing leadership responsibility was because I had witnessed firsthand the value that ERGs can bring, both to the individual and the corporation. ERGs help foster an environment of diversity and inclusion that also brings the following:

Diversity of thought. There's a plethora of research that shows diverse teams are more productive, more innovative, and more financially successful. I have seen this firsthand as a manager —I don't want a team that all thinks the same way. I much prefer a team that approaches problems from different angles, because it means we're more likely to come to the best solution together. I don't want to hire people all from the same college with the same degree—in fact I prefer to hire for a team in which the skills of each person complement each other. Our differences truly do make us stronger. When leadership proves that your voice matters and will be heard, this in turn helps to create…

A culture of belonging. When leadership fosters an environment in which everyone is welcome—and proves that all voices matter and will be heard—people feel welcome to show up as their authentic selves. This creates a workplace culture of belonging, which is at the root of feeling connected to our colleagues. Once we have established a culture of belonging it's then time to think about how we grow, which we do through…

Talent attraction and retention. Intentionally creating a culture of diversity and inclusion fuels the ability to retain talent, which in turn creates the ability to attract new talent. Our ERGs have worked closely with our recruiters to write inclusive job postings, participate in interview panels, and ensure voices are heard and advocated for during the interview process. Talent retention is fostered by ensuring talent has opportunities to grow, which they access through a…

Career development and leadership pipeline. The ERGs in which I've been involved have all offered tremendous opportunities for their members and allies to benefit from career development activities and programming. What I have seen work very well for many people is offering programming that allows members and allies to learn of other's stories, typically career journeys. How did Naomi make the jump from Product Management into Sales and why? How did Bryant get his promotion to Vice President last year? What were the sacrifices they made and who was their mentor to help them get there? Additionally, many ERGs provide coaching and mentoring for their members, and requests for mentorship are their number-one request. People want to grow in their careers, and mentorship can provide the avenue for that advancement. In fact a key factor in talent retention is whether career development opportunities are provided. Our ERGs have also produced the future leaders of our companies, where we are well known for creating a bench of talent for future leadership roles.

Philanthropic giving. Research also shows that employees want a sense of meaning and a sense of purpose in their work. ERGs can provide this as well, by advancing the social causes that are important to the members of the ERG. By offering the opportunity for employees to give back to their own local communities in a volunteer capacity, companies are growing their social impact in ways that are meaningful to their employees.

WHAT IF YOUR company doesn't offer ERGs yet? Getting started doesn't need to be complicated. When I was a co-founder of an ERG it was literally three coworkers and I who got together and decided we wanted to create something to support each other. In less than two years that grew from the four of us to 123 people. It was an exciting time to build something that would be so helpful to so many. I recommend finding others that are passionate about the cause, whatever that may be.

Showcase and highlight the benefits of ERGs to your company's leadership team to find an executive sponsor. In our first several years our ERG operated with no budget—every event was put on by volunteers.

These are some of the decisions you will need to make:

1. **Determine your cause or purpose.** Be very clear on the intention of your group—what are its commonalities and what mission will it advance?
2. **Identify an executive sponsor.** Find a senior leader who is supportive of your cause and who will advocate for your group is paramount for success. In the early days of our first ERG, we invited our executive sponsor to speak at the beginning of every event, which showcased the importance of the group's mission.

3. **Determine a meeting location and frequency.** In-person or virtual? If the meetings are to be in person, where will they be held? We also began with quarterly events and eventually moved to monthly.
4. **Create focus areas**. Our focus areas were networking, career development, and social impact. Our events then revolved around these focus areas.
5. **Determine your budget**. Do any of these events have a cost behind them? How do you request budget from your leadership team? If requesting budget, you'll need to highlight the value the ERG will bring back to the company. Our initial value proposition was in bringing more diverse candidates into our hiring and recruiting cycles. Your executive sponsor should be able to help you formalize the budget request.
6. **Find volunteers**. Who will volunteer to lead efforts? Our initial group of volunteers were given leadership titles based on their area of interest, at least in the beginning! The graphic designer in the group became our communications chair and spearheaded the monthly newsletter, for example.

That's it! That's all you need to get started with your very own ERG.

I have benefited both personally and professionally from being an individual participant in ERGs. I have had new career opportunities open to me, as I was exposed to people and roles in other parts of the organization. I have made genuine friendships from my time in them and I have become a more compassionate and empathic human because of what they've taught me.

So we've seen how these relationships offer support and provide connections that create a sense of belonging and empowerment. Whether they are called ERGs, wellness groups, or affinity groups, they provide corporate benefits too. I am a stronger leader and a better human because of my involvement with ERGs. I encourage you to get involved with your company's ERGs, and if your company doesn't offer them yet, utilize the tools in this chapter to showcase the benefits that they bring.

More important than anything though, I have found the connections that I most need at work. When my mother passed away, my friends in the ERG were there to support me and created a much different work experience than the one I had in the cubicle farm. I was able to grieve with the support of my colleagues and return to my work when I was ready.

I truly have found more meaning and purpose in my work, and have found a support network in forging strong connections with my co-workers.

Wendy McHenry

~

Wendy McHenry is currently the Global Head of Solutions Engineering at CData Software. Across an almost 30-year career in consulting, analytics, and technology, she has led technical teams across several countries spanning different global regions. Wendy is a fierce inclusionist, advocating for diversity of viewpoints and backgrounds, and currently serves as Chairperson of the PreSales Collective Women in Solutions Excellence ("WISE") Council, and on the board of two nonprofit organizations.

Searching Within

Until you make the unconscious conscious, it will direct your life and you will call it fate.

Carl Jung

TWENTY-ONE

Following the Heart's Guidance: A Journey

Weike Lu

It was early summer in Beijing, China in 2004. Lao Xiao was my boyfriend at the time and he and I had just moved into the new home we had bought together. I had worked in advertising media for several years, enjoying flexible hours and a generous income, but I had lost interest in the job. So I was taking a break and looking for a new direction in life. Lao Xiao, who is ten years older than me, was an investment manager at a large company. He had been working there since graduating from college and was well-liked by colleagues and friends.

I met Lao Xiao while hiking with an outdoor adventure organization. Our parents had already met and although we hadn't obtained a marriage certificate, we all knew we would go through the legal process sooner or later. Traditionally, Chinese men take pride in supporting their families but Lao Xiao saw himself as an open-minded man.

When I told him that I wanted to take a break to find meaning in my life, he didn't quite understand. But he still told me, "You don't have to worry about supporting the family. Take a good rest and do what you like. If you want to go back to school for further studies I will fully support you."

Despite our divorce a few years later, I remain grateful to this day for the sense of security he gave me at that time, which allowed me to explore and take risks without worries.

Soon after my conversation with Lao Xiao, I announced my decision to go to India to study yoga. It was a choice that clearly surprised him, but as an open-minded Chinese man he did not try to stop me.

I was away for three months, and during that time I experienced a profound spiritual awakening. Not long after I returned, I shared an even more shocking piece of news—I wanted to create a well-being center.

This sparked nightly discussions with me, Lao Xiao, and the couple downstairs, Yaya and Shitou. The four of us had purchased our home and started renovations at the same time. I am not sure exactly when it began, but despite having different surnames, we developed a close and symbiotic relationship. We discussed almost everything together and became as close as family.

Every day, around late afternoon, the anticipation of our discussions would make my heart beat faster.

Ding, ding, ding, ding.

The clock struck four times one afternoon and Lao Xiao was about to come back from work. Without thinking, I put my hand on my chest hoping to calm my racing heart. I took a deep breath and exhaled slowly, silently reminding myself to stay mindful. The L-shaped floor-to-ceiling window in the living room faced southeast, and I can still feel the warmth of the evening sun. I walked barefoot on the white marble floor, and the stone surface was slightly warm. I laid out the meditation cushion and lit a piece of Indian sandalwood with a lighter. A puff of green smoke rose, and the silky, warm scent suddenly transported me back to the crowded, noisy streets of India. I took another deep breath, refocused my thoughts to the center of the meditation cushion, and slowly sat down.

The new leather sofa in the living room and the aroma of sandalwood together exuded a sense of refined taste. Aunt Wang, the housekeeper who came to clean our home three times a week, was someone we relied on to keep everything in order. Cleanliness and tidiness created the illusion of complete control over one's life. The huge room was quiet, with only the ticking of time passing. I believed that I should always maintain inner joy, peace, and contentment. At least most of the time. Yet inexplicably I felt uneasy and found myself missing that mysterious, chaotic place once again —the happiness on the faces of those who prayed devoutly by the Ganges in the early morning, the physical exhaustion and spiritual contentment after sweating profusely in yoga practice…

Click.

My heart tightened as I heard the sound of the door lock being opened. I immediately returned from my Indian dream to my home and quickly stood up to put away the cushion.

"Are you meditating, Dear?" Lao Xiao came into the room and said, washing his hands. "I can't sit still; you are amazing. Ready to go?"

"Where to?"

"Our canteen," Lao Xiao replied with a smile. "Yaya just called me and said she will cook for us tonight."

"Ah, seeing each other every day—it's not annoying?" I tried to suppress my resistance.

"Yaya said dinner is ready. Doesn't that save you the trouble of cooking?" Lao Xiao dragged me toward the door. I knew I couldn't avoid this predicament so I silently followed him.

Yaya, Shitou, and Lao Xiao were all around the same age. Yaya ran an outdoor club and Shitou was a well-known interior designer. They had met and gotten married through outdoor sports. The three seemed to have a tacit understanding of many things.

We went downstairs. When Shitou opened the door he looked at Lao Xiao, who was dressed in a suit, and gave him a sly smile: "Hey, Mr. Xiao, please come in. Are you here to inspect our work?"

"Okay, cut it out!" Lao Xiao nudged Shitou aside and we walked in.

"It's time for dinner!" Despite her small frame Yaya's voice was clear and loud, drawing everyone to the table.

The colorful dishes on the table were mouthwatering. As we ate, everyone toasted and enjoyed the meal, but I remained inattentive. I hoped the three of them would take my ideas seriously today.

"Duo Duo," Yaya called my nickname, holding the wine glass as she looked at me. "We have visited many places together over the past few days. The locations you like are not cheap. Even a well-run ordinary club takes at least nine months to a year to break even. Your concept of a Well-being Center is so cutting-edge that it will take even longer to build a customer base."

Lao Xiao added in agreement: "Most of the property owners in our community are young and open to new things. However, when I recently asked some neighbors in our building, none of them knew what yoga or meditation was."

"The cost of interior decoration with the Japanese Zen feeling you want will not be low." Shitou also joined the conversation.

I suddenly felt myself shrinking, as if I had returned to my childhood. My father and stepmother had never truly listened to me. They held me hostage under the banner of love and made hypocritical decisions for me that I resented.

"Stop talking! That's enough!" I snapped, glaring at the three of them. "Don't act so superior. You're just a few years older than me." I slammed my hand on the table and stormed out.

I went home alone and headed straight to the bathroom, turning the shower on full blast, hoping the warm water would wash away my anger. "No one takes my ideas seriously," I said to myself.

I spent the next few days on my own, meeting with various potential partners and investors, but it seemed their concerns mirrored those of the three.

I began to re-examine the pleasure that dopamine brought me whenever I sought to realize the meaning of life and my dreams. The last conversation with the four of us had also left a scar of disrespect that was triggered by the shadow of my childhood.

After a few days of cooling off, the small part of me that had curled up in that remote corner slowly stood up. Although I didn't see a clear path ahead, I had a vague sense that my dream was not far away.

Following the Heart's Guidance: A Journey

It was Friday again, and I took the initiative to call everyone and invite them to dinner at a newly opened restaurant in Houhai, a famous tourist attraction in Beijing. Surrounded by temples and the former residences of notable figures, Houhai was centered around three lakes. The area was lively at night, with many newly opened bars and theme restaurants lining the waterfront.

After dinner we took a walk along the closest lake. Without realizing it, we wandered into a quiet spot by the water.

"Well," I cleared my throat. "I have something to say." Everyone stopped walking.

"Sorry for being stubborn last time." I said sincerely, looking at everyone.

"It's okay, we understand. We just wanted to help," they replied in unison.

I then shared my reflections on my childhood experiences and my recent experiences with potential business partners and investors. I told them that I realized how important they were to me, and that I was willing to take their advice seriously—but I also needed them to respect me and treat me as an equal.

Suddenly the crowd around me faded away and the wall between me and the three of them disappeared.

Soon after, with Lao Xiao's help, I rented a nearby studio as an independent investor. Shitou helped me complete the renovations at minimal cost and Yaya guided me in successfully promoting my yoga studio—adapted from my original concept to make it more accessible to the public—through the online platform for our community home owners. In less than three months I broke even and made a profit. A year later I had built my own team of teachers.

I achieved my dream at the lowest cost and I am very grateful that I neither clung stubbornly to my own views nor abandoned my dreams to please others. Instead I grew beyond my own limitations to connect with others.

Thich Nhat Hanh says: "If you don't communicate well with yourself, you cannot communicate well with others. When you can truly … listen to yourself, you can profit from every moment given you to live."

. . .

Twenty years later, I now live in Canada, am a mother of two, and I'm studying in an IMBA program hoping to discover a new direction for the next stage of my life.

The person I am today has gone through periods of solitude—a transcendental spiritual experience in the Buddhist sense—as well as the dark night of the soul. Many years of study and work in individual and group counseling have helped me develop better self-awareness and reflection skills. My practice and teaching of yoga and meditation have allowed me to build a good relationship with my body and mind. But through it all I remain human.

At the end of last year, I planned to set up an online mindfulness meditation group. But with English not being my native language, the clash between Eastern and Western cultures, and the challenge of returning to the workplace after being a full-time mother, I felt deeply powerless. My inner critic kept whispering to me, and once again I felt the familiar sense of insignificance. This time my online co-host Eva became the new threat in my old story.

Once again, I patiently sat with the little girl hiding in the corner until I gathered the courage to share my inner struggle with Eva honestly.

"I understand how you feel. English is not my native language either," Eva said gently. She lives in Germany. "You don't have to face this alone. Let's tackle it together!"

Now our mindfulness meditation group is up and running, and it is going even better than I had expected. Through this experience, we have not only strengthened our mutual trust and friendship but also deepened our enthusiasm and sense of responsibility in our work.

Please don't let your fear rob you of your initiative. Don't let your ego stand in the way of achieving your dreams. To listen to others wholeheartedly is to listen to yourself.

Finally, may you always be in tune with your inner guidance. May you transcend boundaries and become one with the universe.

And may you realize that every person on earth possesses this superpower.

Your heart knows the way. Run in that direction, Rumi says.

Are you ready, my dear friend? Let's run.

Weike Lu

∽

Weike Lu has an extensive background in meditation, having practiced as a nun at Sayadaw U Pandita's Forest Monastery. She participated in the filming of the Indian documentary series "Ganges Stories" and serves as a Mindfulness Meditation Mentor (MMT). In addition, she's an Existential Group Therapist, Satir-Based Family Therapist, Reiki Master, Massage Therapist, and Yoga Teacher. She currently studies at IMBA and resides in Montreal, Canada.

TWENTY-TWO

Common Ground Isn't That Common

Rohit Sawhney

"Yes, almost done—the meeting just finished!" I yell to my mom as I pop my head up slightly over the glow of my MacBook Air.

She's in the kitchen just outside my door. The strong smell of onions, tomatoes, and spices permeates through. She is making one of my favorites, bhartha, fire roasted eggplant mash. The aroma of warm chapathis cooking on the tava, a traditional metal pan, is a comforting symphony of scents. It brings me back, but it also distracts! *Focus and finish,* I say to myself. *You didn't come all this way just to work.*

I prop myself up further on my sit bones, raise my neck, and pull my shoulders back. I'm trying to get comfortable on this four-legged embroidered wooden chair that's tucked under a small desk in the spare bedroom of my grandma's two-bedroom condo. I'm a few miles south of Daytona Beach, Florida. It's been a long day. I took the red eye, with a connection.

I'm desperately trying to wrap up this Webex chat with my manager, who pinged me after our meeting. It's 6 p.m. here, but not for her. I hoped to take this last call and move onto dinner and time with my family. And who enjoys cold homemade food, anyway? It's a delicate balance, especially when communicating through a messaging app, where tone and nuance easily get lost—not my preference. And our relationship is only a few months new. I'm thanking my manager for allowing me to take this last-minute trip cross-country to visit my ailing grandmother as she battles Stage 4 lung cancer. I mention I'm about to sign off. She finishes her thoughts on the meeting then shifts to empathizing.

"Rohit, I know how you feel. I have an aunt who recently passed away from cancer."

I freeze. How can she know how I feel? Her words linger, unsettling. My Nani is my mother's mom (if you are familiar with Indian culture you knew that). She turned 90 years old six months ago. Just last summer the family gathered to celebrate life with cake and a poolside party. Then the news: advanced cancer. My mom and uncle made the selfless decision to take turns providing 24/7 care for Nani, ensuring she wouldn't have to go elsewhere—Asian family values on display. I am the oldest grandchild. She still somewhat recognized me this afternoon when I arrived.

My Nani is still here—still fighting. This isn't the same, I think to myself feeling frustrated, fatigued, and famished all at the same time.

The comment doesn't sit well with me. Not then, not now. How someone feels is deeply personal and unique. As both a manager and, more importantly, a human being, I've learned that true sympathy comes from acknowledging the situation and offering genuine support. But I get it. She is trying. We're not there yet. I can't tell someone what the right thing is to say at the right moment. I reply "thank you" to keep it short in the hope of moving on. In the background I can hear my mom speaking Hindi, offering Nani food as she removes it from the stove. *"Raita khana hai?"* she asks warmly to check if Nani wants homemade yogurt with diced cucumber and seasoning to complement the meal.

I do! I think to myself. I want to be there.

Ding! Another message from my manager.

Common Ground Isn't That Common

I pause. Inhale—one, two, three, four.

Hold—one, two, three, four, five, six, seven.

Exhale, slow through pursed lips—one, two, three, four, five, six, seven, eight.

Four-seven-eight, a reset. A moment to steady myself. I'm ready. I glance down.

"Rohit, I'll need your help to drive this project. Heads up. There's a last-moment meeting today—it's one the VP is calling for."

My stomach tightens. I shake my head left to right vigorously then lean in, scanning the words again and hoping I misread them.

"What?!"

My voice escapes in a whisper, sharp with disbelief. A storm brews in my mind—frustration, confusion, irritation—all colliding in real time like the cloud-based messaging app I'm stuck using for this conversation. The message stares back at me, its weight sinking in. A last-moment meeting? Now? She knows why I'm here. She knows this trip is brief, that my grandmother—my Nani—is slipping away. Just minutes ago she tried to empathize. And now this?

My fingers hover over the keyboard. I want to respond, to push back, to make it clear what this moment means to me. But all I can think is *What the fuck?!*

I think to myself, *Perhaps I shared too much? Or not enough?* I begin to regret not taking a few days off instead of trying to balance work and life. I was trying to help, to be a good team player. I thought we were beginning to establish common ground. She's from Iran; I too was born there and left during the Revolution. We talked about it. Even moments ago, despite the awkward phrasing, it still felt like a moment of understanding. *So I thought.*

WORKPLACE CONNECTION IS TRICKY. We often bond over school, origin, hobbies, family, kids, vacation. "Oh, you're a fan of lumpia too? Let me tell you about…" These small connections are universal. We are wired for them. In person they happen organically

—hallway conversations, lunch breaks, pre-meeting banter. Even remotely we have Zoom breakouts, Kahoot! games, Slido polls. These moments break up the day and make work more human.

But most of these connections remain at the surface. Just like social media friends and followers, they only go deep if we allow them to. True connection happens when we share our respective stories. When we go beyond small talk to understanding *why* someone shows up every day. What drives them? Where are they on their journey? Are they happy with what they have or are they working towards what they want? Both can be true. Who lifts them up or pulls them down? Most importantly, is this reciprocated? Are they curious to understand the answers to these questions about you? Do they listen and show compassion for your journey? In short, do you *get* them, and do they *get* you?

This is where the real magic happens.

Sometimes all you have to do is listen, and the stories unfold whether you've asked for them or not. I have found this incredibly valuable. It's like the blink test—you quickly gain insight into the other person, often more than you realize in those first few moments. It's helped me quickly distinguish whether someone genuinely wants to connect or just needs something from me. This clarity reveals who is an advocate and a true partner, and who is not. Who can I trust when I am not around? Who could I invite to a long meal, where the conversation goes beyond just work?

When it comes to friendships and meaningful connections, a local Bay Area sports radio legend would often pose this question: "Could you see yourself driving cross-country with this person?"

My wife has a similar take—she talks about the kind of friends who feel like family, the ones you can eat crab with (she grew up in Maryland, so blue crab in case you're wondering). It's like breaking bread but stretched over hours—newspaper covering the table, the pinch of Old Bay seasoning under your fingernails, lightly oaked Chardonnay flowing. The best connections are the ones that feel effortless, not forced.

Here is an exercise: Close your eyes. Think about a colleague you've shared more than a handful of meals or drinks with. Was it always about work? Did it go deeper? If not, why not?

But here is a challenge I have often faced. How much sharing is too much? And with whom? Your boss? Peers? Direct Reports? Can you truly bring your full self to work or must you draw a line?

I coached both my daughters in youth sports for ten consecutive years. After losses I would often say to our team, "Sometimes we win; other times we learn." That conversation with my boss was a learning moment, a deduction if we were keeping score (we're not, and I don't). There were other such moments. No surprise. But that conversation stayed with me. It wasn't about ill-intent—it was about the limits of professional empathy. Some relationships stay purely transactional no matter how much effort we put in. Without trust the foundation is shaky at best. It's better to recognize that early. Ironically it's a lot like building products in tech. You need a solid platform to scale, a willingness to experiment, and the insight to fail fast until you find the right fit.

But for me it goes even deeper. Values matter. If an environment doesn't respect my core values—family, service, and faith—it's not the right place for me.

Ten years ago I worked at a gaming company in Palo Alto. We had just moved into Facebook's old headquarters, riding high with the number one game on the App Store and a Super Bowl ad with Kate Upton (riding a horse!). Our team worked hard. Some commuted from San Francisco, making long days the norm. I lived locally but balanced family and coaching duties. On certain days we left early. Work got done, and then some.

One day, the COO walked past our desks at 4 pm, found it mostly empty, took a picture, and sent it to the CEO. I had shared my coaching commitments with leadership—they mattered to me, so I made time for them. But as with personal sharing, it can backfire. Perception of lack of commitment crept in. I've seen it before—team members have shared that it's better to keep your head down, deliver, and stay quiet. Maybe. Or maybe it's just not the right environment. By sharing, you gain insight into who truly supports you and who doesn't—and that awareness can shape your next move.

FINDING TRUE CONNECTION TAKES EFFORT. It's rare, but it's worth chasing. Why? Because when you find it, you can be your true authentic self. You can share how you really feel, what you're going through, and what you need in the moment. You can trust that someone will listen. No judgement, no self-interest. Just presence.

Bringing your whole self to work means navigating these nuances carefully. It means knowing when to be open, when to listen, and when to protect parts of yourself. Work is transactional but relationships within work don't have to be. A manager can be more than just a task-giver and a peer can be more than just a meeting participant in a box on the left corner of your screen.

It's not easy. As with most things in life that truly matter, it must be earned. But when you find it, its impact lasts until long after the work is done.

Having spent decades across different industries and cultures, I've realized how rare true workplace connection can be. The moments that stand out aren't just the big milestones, but the relationships built in-between. It's always about the people and the culture.

Joining a colleague in Seoul as they volunteered at their local church, paddleboarding at sunrise off the coast of Tel Aviv, swapping stories on train rides through Europe—these moments made coworkers feel like friends. Until maybe they fade, or someone leaves, and you don't keep in touch. Because relationships—real ones—take work.

I keep my true connections limited. It's intentional. Some people just get it. And you feel it. Not everyone will reciprocate. And that's okay. It's a selective process.

Common ground isn't that common. So identify who in your workplace truly sees you. Test the waters. Share something real and observe the response. And remember, if a workplace's culture doesn't align with your values, embrace the clarity that provides to seek environments in which you can truly thrive. As the band Coldplay wisely puts it, "If you never try, you'll never know—just what you're worth."

You are worth it. When you find that rare common ground, you'll know. And knowing makes all the difference.

Rohit Sawhney

~

Rohit Sawhney is a product management leader with over 25 years of experience in Silicon Valley across Semiconductors, SaaS, and Cybersecurity. At Palo Alto Networks he helps keep the world secure. A dedicated husband for more than half his life, he's a proud dad to two amazing teen daughters and a mischievous maltipoo. An avid traveler, runner, and drummer, he's always moving, always tapping, and making the most of every moment.

TWENTY-THREE

What Remains After We Hand In the Badge

Nicholas Whitaker

Most of us spend more time with our coworkers than our own families, yet somehow work can be one of the loneliest places we navigate.

We're told to keep things professional, to maintain boundaries, to not get too close. HR manuals and LinkedIn thought-leaders remind us that colleagues aren't family—and they're right. The whole "we're like a family" slogan turns toxic fast when used unconsciously or manipulatively. It blurs boundaries, creates unhealthy expectations, and leaves people burned out and disillusioned.

But does that mean we have to keep relationships at arm's length? Are we doomed to always be looking over our shoulders, keeping our cards close, and avoiding "bringing our whole selves to work" because it isn't safe? I don't think so. And if you're reading this book I bet you don't either.

What if the people we work with could truly see us, and we them? What if they were the ones who helped us navigate challenges at work and beyond—advocating for us, pushing us to grow, reminding us of who we are when the job tries to flatten us into something else? What if we could engage with each other as full and complex humans rather than treating one another as transactional cogs in a machine?

This book is about that question—the messy, complicated, deeply human ways we build community at work. Are we just colleagues or can we be something more? And if we can, what happens when the job ends?

For me that question became real when I found myself struggling with anxiety and burnout in a job that on paper should have been a dream. What got me through wasn't a program or a policy. It wasn't even my direct teammates. It was a hand-picked group of incredible humans I might never have met if not for our shared interests and desire to find real community—at work.

They saw me, listened, and reminded me I wasn't alone. Some of them I still talk to regularly, years after we all stopped working at the company that brought us together. This chapter is a piece of that story—how I went looking for support at work and found something deeper than I expected. It's part of what led me to co-found *Changing Work*, to create spaces where deeper and more conscious relationships could thrive. Humans supporting humans.

If you've ever questioned whether meaningful relationships at work are possible, or if you've felt the sting of losing touch with people you once saw every day, or wondered what happened to those "work besties" after you left—you're not alone. Because in the end it's not about the job. It's about the community we build that lasts long after we've turned in our badge.

Ask Me About Blue Dot, that badge said.

"Hello, my name is Nicholas. I'm one of the organizers of this group and… I struggle with anxiety and panic attacks. I probably have undiagnosed Post-Traumatic Stress Syndrome and burnout."

I look slowly around the room and notice a mix of people meeting my gaze while others stare at the collection of pens and "ideation" tools in the middle of the conference room table.

"Anyway, I don't know. I'm exploring this in therapy, and it's helping, but I believe that we shouldn't suffer quietly and alone. The more I talk about my experience, the more I'm learning that there's a lot of benefit to being supported by community. I couldn't find a space to talk about what it's like to struggle with mental health at work, so I'm happy to be here with you all today."

These were the words that tumbled out of my mouth for the first time in a group setting. I had shared bits and pieces of this with my wife, my closest friends, and my therapist, but I had never dared to utter these words at work before. I didn't feel safe.

It was 2018, still a few years before the pandemic would send us all home. Still a few years before a dozen people I knew at work would experience crippling mental health issues and burnout—before a corporate culture struggling to keep up with the needs of its employees would fall further behind. Many of us, including myself, made the necessary but painful decision to take mental health leave just to recover.

I started this group after a few conversations with people in my office who signed up to talk with me as one of the Blue Dot Listeners. It was a global program that trained people to actively listen to colleagues—not to give advice, not to play therapist. Our main goal was to make it okay to not be okay. We had Blue Dots on our badges and computers that read, "Ask me about Blue Dot," and people did.

Over time that grassroots program became more institutionalized and was absorbed into HR. With that change came more restrictions and reporting requirements that didn't work for everyone. People didn't always trust HR to operate in their best interests so, even though we were volunteers, the association with a program sponsored by HR became a barrier.

When the official program became even more bureaucratic and less trusted, I found myself craving another space in which honest connection could happen more freely. Some of us in the local office started to meet informally. We booked a conference room after hours, went around the room to share our experiences with mental health at work, navigating our Employee Assistance Programs, and discussing other options like therapy, medication, and short-term disability. A common thread was the impact of big tech's fast-paced, chaotic, and often stressful workplace culture on our mental health and well-being—and what we were doing about it.

In March 2020 we had our last in-person meeting before we were all sent home to work from our new business-as-usual.

This shift did not impact us all equally.

We continued to meet via Google Meet but soon people were stretched to their limits—back-to-back video calls, the stress of a global pandemic, and fumbles by a leadership team that wasn't prepared for such a monumental shift in how we worked. I was still a year away from my own breakdown and while I lost this support community a new one started to take its place.

By this time I was increasingly focusing my free time on deepening my mindfulness and meditation practice. I discovered the power of mindfulness to help with workplace stress and anxiety—but I hadn't anticipated the community and sense of belonging that would come with it.

I had just started on a new team when the world began to shut down. I didn't really know anyone and didn't understand the norms. It felt cliquey at times, often cut-throat—always ambiguous. Having transferred from a sales and partnerships team to HR, I was a fish out of water culturally—or more like a fish in my own tiny fishbowl.

The smallest and darkest room in my house had become my office, where I spent at least eight hours a day on a computer, five to six days a week.

But in many ways my experience in the meditation community felt like an evolution of what I had experienced with Blue Dot and our office's informal mental health discussion group. Blue Dot was a group of people who had intentionally set aside part of their day to be self-aware and connected to their inner experience, and to be of service to each other and the broader company.

I found myself drawn deeper into our company's meditation community, gPause, and just before the world shut down I trained as a facilitator of Search Inside Yourself (SIY)—a mindfulness-based program born inside the company that later spun off into its own business. The people I trained with became more than colleagues—we became a sangha, supporting each other as facilitators of both SIY workshops, guided meditations for gPause, and much more.

As the pandemic ramped up, and with it the dysfunction and

stress of a company in crisis mode, many of us felt the need to offer more to our colleagues. A team of volunteers, led by an amazing program manager who advocated for us, worked together to formalize, systematize, and expand the gPause program in response to the new work-from-home reality. Over a few months we united a scattered network of worldwide mindfulness facilitators, trained them, and helped them connect with others searching for community. Eventually we connected and served more than 5,000 colleagues across the globe.

Not only did we have regulars who attended our sessions, but we also had each other.

As the year went on, my relationships with my manager and upper leadership team deteriorated and my connection with some of my teammates became even more strained. People were slipping into survival mode and the cracks in our organizational culture were starting to show.

I was burned out, emotionally depleted, physically broken, and unsure of my next step. A bad reaction to a medication sent me into an anxiety and panic spiral that lasted weeks, maybe months. My performance started to slip but I found it nearly impossible to get the support or guidance I needed from my managers. Eventually I made the decision to protect my mental health by stepping away.

When I finally took a leave of absence it wasn't my direct teammates who checked in on me during those three and a half months. It was my meditation community—fellow teachers, SIY facilitators, and gPause members. These were the people who had witnessed my struggles before I had even fully acknowledged them myself. They reminded me that I wasn't alone, that we were there for each other.

To this day we meet up about once a quarter. Most of us have left or been laid off from the company but we still stay connected. One of my closest friends from that group—someone I've never met in person—still hops on a call with me almost every week. We crack each other up, talk about entrepreneurship, and reflect on how we can be of service to the world.

I still get occasional messages from former regulars of my

guided meditations and workshops. No one ever reaches out to tell me how much a spreadsheet or deck I presented to leadership impacted them, but they all remember how I showed up for the mindfulness community during a challenging time.

What I take away from that period isn't about a program, a job, or even a company. It may sound clichéd, but for me it really was about the people. The ones who saw me, who held space, who reminded me that we didn't have to go through it alone. Long after we moved on from the company, those relationships remained.

I believe it is possible to have friends at work, but they may not always be on your team. Sometimes they emerge from a chosen group of people who share your experience and values—people we find in moments of struggle who create something lasting beyond the walls of the company.

Work relationships can be transient—shaped by projects, restructures, and layoffs. But real friendships—the ones rooted in shared experience, mutual care, compassion, and self-awareness—can outlast the jobs that first brought us together.

In the end it's not about where we work. It's about the communities we foster and choose while we're there.

A call to action

IF THERE'S one thing I've learned it's that work is rarely just about the work. It's about the people we cross paths with—some fleeting, some life-changing. It's about those moments when someone really sees us, when we step up for each other in ways no job description could ever capture. It's about the communities we choose to build, even in places that don't always make it easy.

But meaningful relationships at work don't happen by accident. They require intention, trust, and sometimes a bit of courage. Many of us have been burned before—by toxic cultures, false promises, or friendships that didn't survive the next reduction in workforce. That kind of experience can make it hard to open up again and to believe that real connection is possible.

Yet time and time again I've seen people find their people—whether in an informal after-hours group, a meditation community, or simply in those coworkers who become something more. I've seen how work can be more than just a place we clock in and out of. It can be a place where we grow, where we support each other, where we build friendships that last far beyond the walls of an office.

We are all grappling with the same questions: *Who are we to each other at work? Can we be more than colleagues? And if we can, how do we cultivate those relationships in a way that feels real, supportive, and sustainable?*

I invite you to reflect on your own experience. *What kind of relationships do you crave at work? Who has been in your corner when it really mattered? What small steps could you take to build or strengthen the kind of community that makes work (and life) more meaningful?*

Because in the end it's not about the job. It's about the people we choose to walk alongside. And sometimes those people aren't just colleagues. They're something much more.

Nicholas Whitaker

∿

Nicholas Whitaker is a conscious leadership advocate and human BE-ing coach, author, and co-founder of Changing Work. After more than a decade in big tech, he now works with high performers and leaders who are ready to live and lead with more clarity, impact, and confidence. His coaching and writing challenge outdated workplace norms and support people in reclaiming their time, energy, and sense of purpose. Through coaching, community, and conversation, he helps people reconnect with themselves, each other, and what really matters.

TWENTY-FOUR

Bonding Over Shared Goals

Shelly Dhamija

I am here!
After months of paperwork, I finally arrive in Silicon Valley with four suitcases containing my 40 years of life in India. Exhaustion from the move is camouflaged by the excitement of attaining my desires.

It's a hot summer day. As I park the car I notice there's no covered parking lot, something I benefitted from back home. As I walk over to the designated team area I look around and notice my colleagues engrossed in their work. It's open seating, similar to the India office. It feels so familiar and yet so different. I look around and there aren't any familiar faces and no one walks over to say hello. The thrill of embarking on a new chapter in life and a new role overpowers my loneliness. I find my designated desk and settle in.

At lunchtime I look around and find some people eating lunch at their desk and others too engrossed in their work. So I feel uneasy asking anyone to join me for lunch. I walk over to the cafe and look around to see a familiar face but find no one I know. Even though I worked with so many of my colleagues in the US from the India office it's surprising I don't see a familiar face. As I look for a table, I see that most of the folks are having working lunch and I'm left to dine alone. Although I have had lunch by myself on numerous occasions, this is the first time it occurred at work.

And the reality hit me: I don't have any friends here.

As I sit in the cafe eating lunch by myself, I feel like a fish from a pond who's landed in the sea. It is so lonely. I wonder if I misinterpreted the politeness of my colleagues as friendship. While working in the India office I consciously made efforts to build relationships, even friendships, with employees in the US office . But sitting in a cafeteria filled with hundreds of people, in an office of thousands of employees, I was all alone. My heart is beating faster, and anxiety makes me wonder if I made the wrong choice.

I somehow manage to finish lunch and walk back to where we all work. I continue to experience feelings of loneliness as I go through my day. I take a moment to breathe and ask myself what I want to do with the situation. I open my calendar and start booking lunch one-on-ones with my stakeholders and teammates. Now that I have taken some action I feel relieved and am able to focus on my work.

As HUMAN BEINGS we are inherently part of a community, but it's our choice to decide which kind. I took community for granted until I moved to the US. Coming from a family-oriented culture to an individualistic culture, it was a huge surprise to find that people must *work* their way into building a community.

We end up spending with our coworkers more than 50 percent of the time that we're awake. Having even one trusted coworker can help prevent feelings of loneliness at work. What I learned is that it's not about avoiding emotions or suppressing them, it's about redirecting those emotions towards the purpose that brings us to work every day. It's then natural to build emotional connections.

As I build these emotional connections, I feel elated that I have friends.

My coworker Joe—who I knew for nine years—worked with me on various projects. He would come to me for all sorts of advice, whether about framing an email for an executive or making career decisions or dealing with difficult situations at work. I was a mentor and a coach to him and above all I treated him as a friend. Feeling confident about the friendship, I called him to share my career aspirations and how he might help. He agreed to help me succeed. A few days later, in a meeting with senior leaders, his behavior and actions seemed in complete contrast to the commitment he made. This pattern repeated for several weeks. Now I was not only unable to grow, I was unable to do my job effectively. I was neither included in conversations nor informed about decisions being made.

This was so frustrating at so many levels but the most critical was that I had lost a friend. I reflect on the journey with Joe as well as others. It hit me that I received help only when my coworkers got their own goals met in the process. It took me a while to accept this situation. A sense of solitude began to manifest.

Yet again I didn't have any friends at work.

But many of my friends started as coworkers. As I reflect on the formation of *those* friendships, the main theme is that we worked towards a shared goal of delivering and creating value. We did not compete against each other, but collaborated to succeed as a team. It's amazing what you can accomplish when you don't care who gets the credit. Over the course of time the strong bond of working for a shared goal organically ended up in beautiful friendships.

Another theme that started to emerge was the impact of my career stage on connecting with my colleagues. It's very easy to make friends during the early stages of one's career, when the focus is on learning and growing. During the later stages, when everyone is in the rat race of climbing the corporate ladder, the same cannot be said. There are fewer senior positions and in the desire to climb and prove one's worth, games get played, information is not freely available, and people may even resort to sharing misinformation.

Not only did Joe and his manager keep me out of the loop, at some point Joe's manager questioned what value I brought to the project. I could clearly see the game being played to eliminate or devalue my role, and as a result I let Joe become the face of the project. What stopped him from being honest with me and have a crucial conversation around what he needed to succeed? Was it his insecurity, or was he influenced by his manager—or was it a combination of both? I will never know.

In today's corporate environment, where most are losing sight of how we can collectively solve problems and grow, how do we find those genuine and meaningful connections? I chose to remain authentic and focus on sharing the honest facts sincerely and compassionately. In the process I stayed true to myself.

It's not easy to always be honest. With Joe and his manager I faced repercussions, and the only choice I was eventually left with was to move on and find another role. Of course this choice isn't always available and sometimes isn't even the practical one. We all need those paychecks!

THE RESEARCH DATA and literature suggest that in a psychologically safe climate people will offer ideas and voice their concerns. It's important for leaders to create psychological safety for their teams so that they'll voice half-finished thoughts, ask questions, and brainstorm out loud.

One of the most incisive statements made by organizational researcher Amy Edmondson on this kind of environment is that while you can mitigate for what is said or heard in meetings, you can't mitigate for what is *not* said or heard.[1] Sometimes a person's best option in that environment is to stay silent—because previously they tried to speak up and were met with dismissiveness or were rebuked or spoken over.

Relationships also work better when there are boundaries. It's worthwhile discussing personal preferences and setting expectations around feedback and conflict with our coworkers. Establishing these norms ensures we can be honest with each other on work-related matters.

I shifted my perspective from wanting to build friendships to simply kindling conversations about how to solve challenges in delivering business outcomes. It wasn't easy to make that shift, as how can you not feel the emotions and passion that come along with any human interaction? But the question isn't, *Are we coworkers or friends?* The real question is: Are we treating our coworkers with the same level of honesty, kindness, and respect that we treat our friends and family with?

Be the change you wish to see in the world, as Mahatma Gandhi has told us. This journey begins with self-awareness, awareness of others, and of the environment we're in. Acceptance of others and the environment, and leading with compassion, help us treat our coworkers with the same honesty, kindness, and respect that we shower on our friends and family.

Bringing our whole selves to work is not about bringing the challenges of our personal lives to work and vice versa, it's about staying true to our core values. When we watch a movie in a theatre we silence our phones and similarly, when we go to work we should silence the need to fulfill private shortcomings. Looking to fill personal voids through work and coworkers is not the path to emotional well-being. Emotional wellness begins with understanding these voids and fulfilling them with self-compassion. Once those voids are filled it's then easier to collaborate and bond with coworkers. Even if a coworker isn't a real life ride-or-die friend, the time and effort spent nurturing bonds with them is essential for long-term success both personally and professionally.

It's a beautiful morning as I park my car in the open parking lot with a smile on my face. I walk towards the designated team area and my coworkers greet me. I now have a choice when it comes to which coworker I might eat lunch with. Yes, I have formed meaningful and genuine bonds with my coworkers.

We are collaborators bonding over shared goals and purpose!

Shelly Dhamija

~

Shelly Dhamija is a friend, mentor, and a life coach. As an Organizational Development professional and engineering-focused leader, she brings a unique mix of people- and engineering mindsets to empower and enable teams to deliver the best solutions and become better versions of themselves. She leads with compassion, embraces life with positivity and grace, and gives back to her community and those around her with a resilient spirit and a warm heart.

TWENTY-FIVE

Fear of Success

Julia Melim Coelho

Every other day in New York City I would see a news story about a train delay because someone jumped in front of the tracks. In one cover story, a photographer captured the moment a man jumped in front of a train as it arrived. Perhaps he could have saved the man's life instead of taking the picture. Another story was about a lonely girl at a party who left a boring conversation mid-sentence and jumped off the roof at a high rise. At around the same time the media was covering the suicides of high-profile celebrities like Robin Williams and Anthony Bourdain.

My own colleague, Jeffrey Slonim—known as The King of the Red Carpet—took his own life by falling onto the Lincoln Center Illumination Lawn.

When something like that happens to someone you know, you overplay your every interaction, wondering what you might have done differently. I knew it wasn't my fault and I didn't know how it was going to hit me, but it did. I imagine he was hiding a pain deep inside that we knew nothing about. Jeff was Julianne Moore's high school date, and he interviewed her years later on the red carpet. That's where our worlds collided. I knew him as the red carpet reporter for *People*, *Allure*, and other outlets. I always admired Jeff and looked up to him.

As an actress I got used to having one persona on stage and another behind the scenes. As a reporter and television host, I had to pretend everything went smoothly even when it didn't and keep smiling at all costs. I believed that having this persona worked, until I realized I had created a life that looked good on the outside but didn't feel good on the inside.

Once, on the red carpet at the Lincoln Center Theater, as we waited for Richard Gere at a premiere at the New York Film Festival, some colleagues, including Jeff, talked about how we would end our lives. We were using humor to deflect the pain we all felt in common. I said I would do it exactly where we were standing, because so many red carpet events happen there. Someone would notice me sooner than if it happened at home and it would make the headlines. My biggest fear was that because I lived alone in a studio apartment it would take a long time for people to find me if I died. Maybe it could take weeks or months. Probably it would be the doorman with a package delivery needing a signature.

I remember noticing that Jeff wasn't acting his usual self the last few times we interacted. He seemed a little off. I offered him sparkling water at one of the events and tried to make conversation, and lighten up the mood, but he wouldn't go along with it. You always second guess yourself, convince yourself you're exaggerating and they'll be just fine. Sometimes they are not fine. We had lunch at an event in the Hamptons and he introduced me to his family and they were lovely. I thought I was probably just being paranoid and let it go.

A few months later I heard the news. He wasn't fine.

At the time that Jeff left this Earth, I was very lonely, depressed, and having suicidal thoughts myself. I honestly don't know anyone who hasn't had them, although we never think anyone will go through with it. I felt that I had achieved most of what I set out for and my goals in life felt meaningless.

My own suicidal thoughts went back a long way. I was raped when I was nineteen years old, on New Year's Eve, and I didn't press charges. I didn't want anyone to know because I was so ashamed. Being raped makes you feel like you're not whole and can never make yourself whole. I was so confident before that and afterwards I shaved my head and moved to a different country. That's how I dealt with my pain, moving as far away from it as possible. When I was 22 I tried to commit suicide. I didn't want to live with that thought in my head haunting me forever.

"I just wanted to go to sleep and not have to worry about any more concerns of the world," is what I said to the therapist, describing how I took sleeping pills to deal with the anguish. My therapist told me I had been through enough trauma and my actions were understandable. I wasn't prescribed any medication and to everyone else I had food poisoning. I felt like I didn't deserve good things in life: happiness, love, success. I knew that in theory I deserved all the good in the world—I knew it wasn't my fault, that I shouldn't let it affect me. But it has affected every area of my life in more ways than I care to admit. And because I didn't want anyone to find out or to share my history of abuse, I punished myself.

After Jeff's death I for the first time in my life had a panic attack. I dedicated so much time to being who I wasn't that even my body wasn't responding. I had to find a way back to being my whole self again. I remember lying on the hardwood floor not able to breathe. I hadn't had the chance to express myself and to be proud of the woman I had become. It takes courage to share a story like mine, it shouldn't feel shameful to admit it, and I needed to get rid of the pain of silence. I wasn't a scared little girl anymore, but there were parts of that girl that were still inside me and scared to come out—and that's okay. I was her but I was so much more, and I wanted to make her shine.

At the same time, I also felt like nothing I did was ever enough and that none of us would ever matter as much as those walking the red carpet. There was something missing behind the spotlight, something that nobody was talking about: the emptiness we all feel, the fear of success, fear of happiness, fear of love, fear of being my full authentic self, feeling like I was never enough.

Fear and emptiness had showed up at work throughout my career.

I once had a boss fire me because he "couldn't have a hot Brazilian girl in his office," even though I was amazing at my job. According to him it was too distracting for his clients and the celebrities, so I couldn't steal the spotlight.

Another boss told me, "You've done so much in the last few years, if you were a man you would definitely be promoted."

Working as a TV producer I could only go to the bathroom if my boss was finished talking.

These seem like sentences out of a playbook of "don'ts" in the workplace, but this is reality. This kind of behavior is not as hidden as you'd like to think.

I DECIDED TO STOP EVERYTHING, take a week off, and go to a yoga retreat in Costa Rica. I hadn't felt that kind of happiness in a long time. Our schedule consisted of waking up early for morning yoga, eating fresh mangoes for breakfast, feeding the squirrels, then going into the ocean at a beach nearby or horseback riding in the rainforest. Our retreat also included meditations, journaling and creative writing—another outlet I needed to explore. Writing has always been a part of my journey and it took me a while until I fully embraced it as my persona. I had been journaling since I was little but my subconscious mind somehow forgot to include that into my daily practice. I had also found a community of writers, yogis, and meditators who were a breath of fresh air.

It was the medicine I didn't know I needed, and I thought maybe the solution was moving to Costa Rica, the happiest place on earth, and adopting their motto: Pura Vida!

That's when I embraced the motto *Feed Your Soul* as my mission in life. For me it's an attempt to help people discover what really feeds their souls—something that lightens up our day and makes life worth living. I found out that many celebrities behind their red carpet persona have a secret passion that keeps them going, something that makes them get out of bed in the morning, completely unrelated to what they're famous for. Once they achieve everything they dream of, they realize it was never about fame and fortune. Hilary Swank is passionate about saving rescue dogs, for example, and that's what keeps her sane. Nonetheless, developing that secret passion is about looking for ways to light up our souls.

I quit drinking on New Year's Eve. I realized that alcohol had played a big part in keeping my mouth shut, like always having a toxic friend nearby, or just saying what others wanted to hear—but never really showing up as my authentic self. This time I had decided to start connecting with others from a heart-centered place. I knew it would come at some cost and that I would lose some relationships. What I didn't realize was that I already had some great friends who supported my authentic self, some of whom I had been neglecting for a long time.

Sometimes it feels impossible to embrace who you are, like there's no solution and you feel like giving in. It's for those moments most of all that we need people who are willing to take a chance and help us take the leap. One of those people for me was my acting teacher and mentor.

"You need to meet Kevin McCorkle," the Program Manager at SAG-AFTRA Brenda Cisneros told me. That was the first time I heard his name.

Working with Kevin gave me the hope that I needed to believe in myself again; he reminded me of everything I still could be. I was not completely lost after all, and he guided me on what to do next— literally gave me a workbook—and even when I didn't believe in myself at first, I started seeing results. He showed up in more ways than I could ever have expected. I realized it wasn't easy finding people who are happy for your success and truly want to support your journey. I started remembering who I was.

Standup comedy was a way to be myself unapologetically, so that became a big part of my life. Once I decided to embrace who I was, doors of opportunity started opening up and I finally received the recognition I wanted without having to hide who I really am. It was scary at first, like when you feel naked and vulnerable in front of an audience. Little did I know that my imposter syndrome wasn't all gone. Now that I was finally able to be myself, that same voice was telling me that I didn't deserve all that, that it was not possible that so many people could love me for who I am, and sooner or later I would fail.

On stage I had the courage to be someone else, but it was still hard showing up as my true self in my personal life and opening up my heart about what really matters. Pushing people away was easier than having heart-to-heart conversations. I thought I could keep that up my entire life, but I knew I needed to have my voice heard and time was running out.

That's the issue with success. Once you have it, you're scared of losing it. Same as love.

Success is about falling deeply and madly in love with yourself. So much so that you have the courage to take the leap, to go for all your dreams, passions, aspirations. Live life as if you only had one day on Earth because you never know when it will be your last. Tell people you love them and cherish every moment. I've changed a lot since I was lying on that hardwood floor.

I've made my own ritual in the mornings, as my personal mantra is *My first hour is mine*. I start the day with meditation, yoga, breathwork, then journaling. And since I started writing again the impossible happened: people started noticing me. I began receiving opportunities that seemed out of reach before and I was being asked to collaborate on so many projects that I felt like I was dreaming. By being myself, I was beginning to be more successful than I had ever dreamed possible. It was about doing what's right for me, without following any formula. All I had to do was show myself to be loved.

I wonder if I'm being irresponsible for sharing this story. This is the chapter I never wanted to share. This is my deepest darkest secret, which I was hoping no one would ever find out. This is the chapter I've been hiding all my life, one whose ugly truths I've been doing anything and everything to conceal. But life is about being brave enough to share your ugly truths. That's the only way out. Sometimes we forget we're human, that we have complexities, and that's what life is all about. I am a complex, loving, passionate, human being. The truth is, if there's any chance I might save someone by sharing this story, then it's worth it. Because in life, if we lose people, maybe we can save them too.

Even in the hard days I found at least one thing that made me happy. I learned to be grateful, and I wrote a love letter to myself. I am deeply in love with myself. This takes radical self-love, a lot of courage, compassion—including self-compassion—and gratitude.

Being yourself is your biggest revolutionary act. Don't wait to become who you think you need to be. Feed your soul now.

Julia Melim Coelho

Julia Melim Coelho is originally from Brazil and received an Inner MBA from Sounds True on Mindfulness and Transformative Business Leadership. Julia is known as the host of CBS' lifestyle show "City Guide" and as the red carpet host for Hollywood TV—where she has interviewed Ryan Gosling, Julianne Moore, Robert De Niro, and George Clooney, among others. She produced a Netflix series with Sylvester Stallone and launched the wellness podcast Feed Your Soul Mixtape.

Notes

7. Building My Home

1. Hall, Jeffrey. (2019). How many hours does it take to make a friend?. *Journal of Social and Personal Relationships* 36, 1278-1296.

13. A Mystery Solved

1. Jay, Shani. "11 Team Effectiveness Models to Build High-Performing Teams." *Academy to Innovate HR*, 2022, www.aihr.com/blog/team-effectiveness-models/.
2. De Jong, Bart A et al. "Trust and team performance: A meta-analysis of main effects, moderators, and covariates." *The Journal of Applied Psychology* 101.8 (2016): 1134-50.

16. Four Questions to Turn Coworkers into Collaborators

1. Doerflinger, Johannes T., Torsten Martiny-Huenger, and Peter M. Gollwitzer. "Planning to deliberate thoroughly: If-then planned deliberation increases the adjustment of decisions to newly available information." *Journal of Experimental Social Psychology* 69 (2017): 1-12.
2. Lin, Xiaoshuang and Herman Tse. "Research: Humble Leaders Inspire Others to Step Up." Harvard Business Review, January 29, 2025.
3. Gallup. "The Relationship Between Strengths-Based Employee Development and Organizational Outcomes," https://www.gallup.com/cliftonstrengths/en/269615/strengths-meta-analysis-2015.aspx, July 2016.
4. Gallup. "Improve Work Performance With a Focus on Employee Development," https://www.gallup.com/workplace/269405/high-performance-workplaces-differently.aspx, January 19, 2024.
5. Rock, David and Heidi Grant "Why Diverse Teams Are Smarter," *Harvard Business Review*, November 4, 2016.

18. GIRLIE, This Isn't a Family Affair!

1. Bennett, Michelle. "Building relationships at work." *Niagara Institute*, February 8, 2024.
2. Mental Health America. "What is emotional intelligence and how does it apply to the workplace?" Undated. https://mhanational.org/what-emotional-

Notes

intelligence-and-how-does-it-apply-workplace.
3. *American Behavioral Clinics.* "10 Signs of emotional maturity." Undated. https://americanbehavioralclinics.com/10-signs-of-emotional-maturity/.

20. Transforming Isolation into Connection: A Practitioner's Guide

1. Bryant, Kalina. "The Impact of Employee Resource Groups in the Workforce." *Forbes*, 16 September 2023, www.forbes.com/sites/kalinabryant/2023/09/15/the-impact-of-employee-resource-groups-in-the-workforce/.

24. Bonding Over Shared Goals

1. Edmondson, Amy C. *The fearless organization: Creating psychological safety in the workplace for learning, innovation, and growth.* John Wiley & Sons, 2018.

Epigraph Citations

Chan, A., ed. *Mencius: Contexts and Interpretations.* Honolulu: University of Hawai'i Press, 2002: 115.

Jung, Carl. Christ, a Symbol of the Self. *Routledge,* 1959: 4.

Krznaric, Roman. The Secret To Finding Meaningful Work. *Pan Macmillan UK,* 2012: 2.

Luther King, Jr., Martin. Oberlin College Commencement, 1965.

Williamson, Marianne. *Return to Love.* Harper Collins, 1992: 27.

About Changing Work

Changing Work is a movement deeply committed to revolutionizing the dynamics of the workplace from within.

Our Vision is to **Change Work from the Inside Out.**

Essentially, we are here to make work a more humane, conscious, and nurturing environment; an experience that promotes personal growth, self-awareness, and compassion, while continuing to deliver value to all stakeholders. We recognize that profitability is important, and that it comes with a need for balance not only for shareholders but also for employees, customers, and the broader global community—a world that works for everyone.

Changing Work is a collective of business leaders, employees, coaches, and consultants. Fundamentally, we do two things:

First, we build community. There's something incredibly powerful about being on a journey together with people who are bonded by a desire for a common good. One of our favorite things is our monthly community meeting. There's so much love in the room!

Second, we share best practices. This comes in many forms, including the book in your hands right now. We also have a podcast, a newsletter, courses, cohort-based learning, and so much more.

Have something you'd like to share? Or something you'd like to learn? Or would you just like to be surrounded by like-hearted people?

Come join us at **www.changingwork.org**

Made in United States
Troutdale, OR
06/03/2025